To Empower People

To Empower People

From State to Civil Society

Second Edition

Peter L. Berger and Richard John Neuhaus

Edited by Michael Novak

The AEI Press
Publisher for the American Enterprise Institute
WASHINGTON, D.C.
1996

This publication, like the seminar from which it springs, is a joint project of the American Enterprise Institute and the Institute for the Study of Economic Culture at Boston University, with the support of the Lynde and Harry Bradley Foundation.

Available in the United States from the AEI Press, c/o Publisher Resources Inc., 1224 Heil Quaker Blvd., P.O. Box 7001, La Vergne, TN 37086-7001. Distributed outside the United States by arrangement with Eurospan, 3 Henrietta Street, London WC2E 8LU England.

Library of Congress Cataloging-in-Publication Data

To empower people: from state to civil society / edited by Michael Novak.—2nd ed.
  p. cm.
  Rev. ed. of : To Empower People / Peter L. Berger.
  Includes bibliographical references.
  ISBN 0-8447-3944-8 (cloth : alk. paper). — ISBN 0-8447-3945-6 (pbk. : alk. paper)
  1. Social Policy. 2. Social institutions. I. Novak, Michael. II. Berger, Peter L. To empower people.
HN18.B459
361.6'1—dc20   95–46026
                                                         CIP

The AEI Press
Publisher for the American Enterprise Institute
1150 17th Street, N.W., Washington, D.C. 20036

Printed in the United States of America

Americans of all ages, all stations in life, and all types of disposition are forever forming associations. There are not only commmercial and industrial associations in which all take part, but others of a thousand different types—religious, moral, serious, futile, very general and very limited, immensely large and very minute. Americans combine to give fêtes, found seminaries, build churches, distribute books, and send missionaries to the antipodes. Hospitals, prisons, and schools take shape in that way. Finally, if they want to proclaim a truth or propagate some feeling by the encouragement of a great example, they form an association. In every case, at the head of any new undertaking, where in France you would find the government or in England some territorial magnate, in the United States you are sure to find an association.

—Tocqueville, *Democracy in America*

Contents

Contributors

MICHAEL NOVAK, the 1994 Templeton laureate, holds the George Frederick Jewett Chair in Religion and Public Policy at the American Enterprise Institute. He is also AEI's director of social and political studies. In 1986, Mr. Novak headed the U.S. delegation to the Conference on Security and Cooperation in Europe. In 1981 and 1982, he led the U.S. delegation to the United Nations Human Rights Commission in Geneva. In 1994, besides the Templeton Prize for Progress in Religion, Mr. Novak was awarded the Wilhelm Weber Prize in Essen, Germany, and the International Award of the Institution for World Capitalism in Jacksonville, Florida. The author of more than twenty-five books, he is also a cofounder and the publisher of *Crisis* and a columnist for *Forbes.*

PETER L. BERGER is director of the Institute for the Study of Economic Culture and professor of economics at Boston University. He is the author of numerous books, including *Invitation to Sociology, The War over the Family,* and *The Capitalist Revolution.* His most recent book is *A Far Glory: The Quest for Faith in an Age of Credulity.*

DOUGLAS J. BESHAROV is a resident scholar at the American Enterprise Institute and a visiting professor at the University of Maryland School of Public Affairs. He was the first director of the U.S. National Center on Child Abuse and Neglect. His most recent book is *Recognizing Child Abuse: A Guide for the Concerned.*

STUART M. BUTLER is vice president and director of domestic and economic policy studies at the Heritage Foundation. In March 1990, he was appointed a commissioner of the Advisory Commission on Regulatory Barriers to Affordable Housing by Housing Secretary Jack Kemp. He is the author of several books, including *Enterprise Zones: Greenlining the Inner Cities,* and coauthor of *Out of the Poverty Trap,* with Anna Kondratas, and, most recently, *A National Healthcare System for America,* with Edmund Haislmaier.

WILLIAM A. GALSTON is a professor in the School of Public Affairs, University of Maryland at College Park, and director of the university's Institute for Philosophy and Public Policy. From 1993 to 1995, he served as deputy assistant to President Clinton for domestic policy. He is the author of six books and numerous articles in the areas of political philosophy, public policy, and American politics. Among his many books is *Liberal Purposes: Goods, Virtues, and Diversity in the Liberal State.*

DAVID G. GREEN is director of the Health and Welfare Unit at the Institute of Economic Affairs. He was formerly a Labour councillor in Newcastle upon Tyne from 1976 to 1981 and a research fellow at the Australian National University in Canberra from 1981 to 1983. He is the author of *Working Class Patients and the Medical Establishment, The New Right: The Counter Revolution in Political, Economic and Social Thought,* and, most recently, *Reinventing Civil Society: The Rediscovery of Welfare without Politics.* He is the coauthor of *Mutual Aid or Welfare State,* with L. Cromwell, and *Medicard: A Better Way to Pay for Medicines?* with David Lucas.

MICHAEL J. HOROWITZ is a senior fellow at the Hudson Institute, where he directs the Project for Civil Justice Reform. He taught civil rights law at the University of Mississippi during the late 1960s and served as general counsel of the Office of Management and Budget during the Reagan administration. He has lectured and written extensively on the subject of legal and constitutional rights.

MICHAEL S. JOYCE is president and chief executive officer of the Lynde and Harry Bradley Foundation. He was previously executive director and trustee of the John M. Olin Foundation. In 1978 and 1979, he was director of the Institute for Educational Affairs and, from 1975 to 1978, director of the Goldseker Foundation. He is a contributing editor of a textbook series in the social sciences and author of numerous studies and articles.

LESLIE LENKOWSKY is president of the Hudson Institute, an adjunct professor of public policy at Georgetown University, and an adjunct scholar at the American Enterprise Institute. Before joining the Hudson Institute in 1990, he was president of the Institute for Educational Affairs. He served as deputy director of the United States Information Agency in 1983 and as director of research at the Smith Richardson Foundation from 1976 to 1983. He is the author of *Politics, Economics, and Welfare Reform: The Failure of the Negative Income Tax in Britain and the United States* and a regular contributor to *The Chronicle of Philanthropy*.

RICHARD JOHN NEUHAUS is president of the Institute on Religion and Public Life and editor in chief of its monthly journal, *First Things*. His articles appear frequently in the *Wall Street Journal* and other national publications. Among his books are *The Naked Public Square, The Catholic Moment,* and *Doing Well and Doing Good*.

MARVIN OLASKY is professor of journalism at the University of Texas at Austin, senior fellow at the Progress and Freedom Foundation, and editor of *World,* a weekly news magazine from a Christian perspective. He is the author of *The Tragedy of American Compassion*.

JAMES P. PINKERTON is a lecturer at the Graduate School of Political Management at George Washington University. He served as deputy assistant for policy planning to the president from 1989 to 1992. He has worked in the Reagan White House and in the past four presidental campaigns. He is the author of *What Comes Next: The End of Big Government and the New Paradigm Ahead* and numerous articles that have appeared in the *Los Angeles Times,* the *New Republic,* the *Wall Street Journal,* the *Washington Post,* and the *National Review*.

WILLIAM A. SCHAMBRA is director of general programs at the Lynde and Harry Bradley Foundation in Milwaukee. He has served as a senior adviser and chief speechwriter for Attorney General Edwin Meese III, Director of the Office of Personnel Management Constance Horner, and Secretary of Health and Human Services Louis Sullivan.

He is the author of numerous articles that have appeared in *The Public Interest, Public Opinion,* the *Wall Street Journal,* the *Washington Times, Policy Review,* and *Crisis* and is the editor of *As Far as Republican Principles Will Admit: Collected Essays of Martin Diamond* (AEI, 1992).

ROBERT L. WOODSON, SR. is president and founder of the National Center for Neighborhood Enterprise. He has been a resident fellow at the American Enterprise Institute and director of the National Urban League's administration of justice division. In 1990 he was awarded the John D. and Catherine T. MacArthur Fellowship for his work in the revitalization of low-income, urban neighborhoods. His writings include *On the Road to Economic Freedom: An Agenda for Black Progress; A Summons to Life: Mediating Structures and the Prevention of Youth Crime* (AEI, 1981); and *Youth Crime and Urban Policy: A View from the Inner City* (AEI, 1981). He is also the author of numerous newspaper articles.

1

Introduction to the 1996 Edition

Michael Novak

T he new and fruitful public policy approaches for the future, Peter L. Berger and Richard John Neuhaus dared to suggest in 1977, do *not* lie in pursuing the lines of attack long beloved of both liberals and conservatives. They lie in taking up a fresh starting place and heading in a new direction.

In this new edition of *To Empower People*, the original text speaks for itself as it has with exemplary power for nearly twenty years. But added to it are eleven freshly minted essays illustrating what has happened to that original argument during the past two decades—how it has spread its roots and branches, involved a variety of scholars in an amazing range of fields, and continued to fascinate practitioners. To these fresh explorations, Berger and Neuhaus provide a thoughtful response.

A New Path of Inquiry

Given its influence, it is hard to believe that *To Empower People* was at its first appearance virtually a *pamphlet*—not more than forty-five pages in length. In the history of political literature, of course, the pamphlet has long played a prominent role. The American Revolution of 1776, for instance, was a pamphleteers' war, the case for independence having been argued for years in sermon-sized booklets designed to define a few new concepts, prod the mind with

1

succinct argument, and enkindle the heart to action. While it was not written so much with passion as with cool analysis, *To Empower People* almost immediately made its presence felt in public policy discussions. Both on the Left and on the Right, the phrase *empowering people* took root. Both on the Left and on the Right, fresh experiments in social action focused on neighborhood groups.

There is no need here to rehearse the original text's argument. The entire pamphlet is reprinted here as part five, exactly as it appeared nearly twenty years ago. The reader will come upon it in its own words momentarily.

What this introduction should first point out, however, is that text's *originality*. *To Empower People* really did change the course of public policy analysis beginning about 1977, even if (as Berger and Neuhaus themselves contend) its basic concepts did not exactly need to be invented by the authors—in separate pieces they had been available in sociological and theological literature for some time. The originality of this important pamphlet lay in two of its predominant features: first, it brought heretofore separate bits of analysis into a concise whole; second, it applied them in a vivid and stimulating way to the dissatisfaction many people—both progressives and conservatives—were beginning to feel with the received wisdom.

To Empower People opened up a new path of inquiry, suggested a new public policy hypothesis, and called for that path of inquiry and that hypothesis to be further tested by others. As the accompanying essays show, this new path of inquiry has proved quite fruitful; its core idea has stimulated many diverse persons. The illuminating power of the hypothesis that "mediating structures" offer the best hope for the future has shed new light on longstanding practical dilemmas. It is often much cheaper, for example, for public policy to allow certain citizens vouchers or tax rebates to provide for special needs on their own rather than to depend on state facilities: care for a retarded child at home, for instance, is far cheaper than state hospitalization.

One reason for the widespread acceptance of the Berger-Neuhaus approach may be as follows. In modern political thought, two terms have until recently tended to dominate discourse: the *individual* and the *nation-state*. This can hardly be surprising, since both these terms (and their underlying realities) are modern arrivals on the stage of history. But these two terms apply, as it were, only to the two extremes of social life, excluding the "thickest" parts of social living in between.

The rise of the *nation-state* came about as heretofore separate petty kingdoms were brought to unity in new and larger national units, as in Germany and Italy in the nineteenth century. Entire populations were suddenly instructed to subordinate their ancient local and regional loyalties to the "higher" loyalty they now owed the suddenly emergent legal order of the "nation." Almost as if in echo, there arose, as well, the sharp awareness among more and more *individuals* (first a few, then others, and finally a great many) that each is an atomic, lonely, and poignantly vulnerable *individual*. Each one may be proud of his or her new independence; but each also had reason in this brave new world to become a little more anxious about his or her personal security, survival, even identity.

Never before had nationalism—and the modern state, which is its lodestar—exercised so broad and highly organized an appeal upon human hearts. Never before had individuals felt so detached from kin and neighbors. Until recent generations, most loyalties had been local, feudal, personal—the fruit of inherited fealties—rather than abstract, legal, and systematized in the new modern style of rationalized bureaucracies, conscripted armies, and impersonal welfare dependencies.

Suffice it to say here that this book's introduction of the term *mediating structures* into public argument is properly singled out as a significant moment in the history of American public policy. Until the appearance of the term, public policy discourse in the United States tended to be pulled toward one of two polar notions: the *individual* or the *state*.

In one frame of reference (the European), these poles attracted, respectively, the liberal *Right* and the socialist or social-democratic *Left*. In another frame of reference (the American), they were the opposite poles around which clustered conservatives to the one side and the liberal-left to the other. Pose a social problem to an American conservative, and the chances were high he would appeal to everything the individual could do for himself, if only the collectivist state would get out of the way. Pose a social problem to an American liberal, and the chances were he would try to invent a new federal program, policy initiative, or agency to tackle it. American conservatives expressed their ideals in terms of "the individual." American liberals liked to describe themselves as "the party of compassion," bringing "an activist government" to the support of the needy.

The Berger-Neuhaus concept of mediating structures suggested that both these approaches had become as outmoded as they were increasingly ineffectual. Both approaches, they said, rested on misdiagnoses of social reality. The new essays in this book carry forward that critique of the old Right and the old Left.

The Arrangement of the New Edition

The new essays accompanying the original text of *To Empower People* grew out of a study group formed to think through this new stage of the argument. They are arranged in four sections. Part one contains two essays, one American and one English, on the intellectual history out of which the concept of mediating structures is now in the ascendant. The first essay, by Michael Joyce and William Schambra, sketches the rise of the twentieth-century "progressive" ideal in the United States: the dream of a new "national" community beyond the "selfish interests" and "parochial concerns" of local communities and regions, led by experts, bolstered by scientific methods. David Green sketches the rather different intellectual history of the rise of the welfare state in Britain, at the expense of the organic ties of traditional communities and associations. The working group explicitly sought an essay from abroad, to suggest the fact that the struggle for a new nonstatist approach to social policy now occupies the energies of many nations.

In part two, James Pinkerton recounts in vivid terms the fascinating "pilgrim's progress" of the new idea of mediating structures in presidential politics from 1977 until the present. From his post in the Bush White House, and as a major chronicler of the history of the idea of empowerment, Pinkerton is one of the saga's key players. William Galston, even in the last furious days of his service in the Clinton White House, found time to join our study group and to put down on paper his own account of how his small band of "new Democrats" in the White House approached the task of reinvigorating the nation's mediating structures.

These are both brief and lively histories. They show the bipartisanship of the idea of mediating institutions. They also show how much easier it is to talk about the idea than actually to find ways of realizing it, especially through the agencies of government. It is worth noting, however, that every White House since the appearance of the Berger-Neuhaus pamphlet has felt the need to cope with mediating structures, even if the typical way of coping has been to mention the idea in speeches, while doing painfully little in practice.

Part three is by far the longest part, containing seven essays dealing with the many varied practical problems that arise in different fields as people try to restore the vitality of mediating structures, as replacements of or supplements to the welfare state. The actual texture of civil society, it turns out, has many faces, set at odd angles to one another. Mediating structures, therefore, do not at all fit the patterns of bureaucratic rationality. They require a more prudential, case-by-case form of reasoning. For one thing, the term *mediating structures* covers an enormous array of different types of institutions. For another, in such structures important circumstances (the character of local leadership, for example) are always shifting.

Thus, what started out as a brief forty-five-page treatment of mediating structures in the Berger-Neuhaus original text has opened up so many diverse and fascinating intellectual problems that our seven essayists here need to deploy three times as many pages. Meanwhile, even these seven essays barely touch on a range of problems still in need of study. For example, despite many efforts, and although some of these problems are hinted at in other essays, we were not able to secure a separate paper on the problems raised for mediating structures by governmental regulation. We had to leave other gaps as well, as astute students will notice. What we did manage to cover, however, was already quite a lot.

Chapters 6, 7, and 8, for example, look at the problems faced by mediating structures in the light of three different sorts of institutions: the law, philanthropy, and religious charities.

Michael J. Horowitz focuses on the constitutional problems that arise from some of the new enthusiasms of the legal establishment during the past thirty years. Of the two conceptual frameworks for thinking about constitutional law, he suggests, the currently dominant vision is a regime of rights, whereas the more traditional vision holds to a regime of contract, custom, and local practice. Without dwelling on the point, Horowitz suggests that certain local agencies of government, such as school boards and local public housing authorities, are in their own way mediating structures. They might not exactly meet the definition given by Berger and Neuhaus, since after all they are in some sense a part of the state apparatus. To the extent that these agencies are subject to local control, though—and until recently they used to be very largely under local control—it seems legitimate enough to think of them as extensions of local communities, with their indigenous customs and practices and tacit systems of accountability, rather than as rote instruments of distant government authorities, obeying abstract bureaucratic rules.

In recent years, however, under the pressure of the new "rights regime," distant authorities began indeed to drive out local control and thus to crush these local "mediating structures." Horowitz makes this case with passion and throws new light on one of the themes first brought up by Joyce and Schambra in their opening essay: the pressure brought by certain progressive elites to nationalize formerly local institutions and, in this case, to do so with the full weight of a new interpretation of the law. The rationale behind this new tyranny has been to help the poor; but the condition of the poor is now in many respects worse than before.

In the next essay, Leslie Lenkowsky details how even the great philanthropic foundations, once thought of as an "independent sector," have slowly been drawn into an indecent liaison with government. Instead of supplying a counterweight to government funding, an alternative, or a set of fresh imaginative options, foundations have frequently been co-opted by the seductive techniques of governmental agencies. As a result, the great philanthropic organizations have become increasingly dependent on government, programmatically homogeneous, and complicit in the growing nationalization of our formerly diverse, independent, and contrarian civic life. They have been betraying their unique identity and vocational possibilities.

In the third essay, Marvin Olasky tells the sad story of the corruption of one highly successful religious charity in Houston and its religious and spiritual decline. Formerly, this was a place where luckless and homeless men turned for moral and religious nourishment and through which they were often "converted"—that is, led to take hold of their lives and turn themselves around, and then to go out the door to face the world on their own. Now having been beguiled into accepting the steady fuel lines of government funding, new and more "professional" officers can say nothing to their charges about religion or morals. They feed them and clothe them as if they were cattle, while being obliged to leave their spiritual lives undisturbed. Thus, this once creative center has now become little more than a warehouse for storing listless human beings.

Robert L. Woodson, Sr., next recounts briefly some neighborhood success stories that have occurred under the inspiration of the turn toward mediating structures. Woodson, a veteran of this twenty-year battle, edited *A Summons to Life: Mediating Structures and the Prevention of Youth Crime* (1981), one of the five volumes for the Mediating Structures and Public Policy project sponsored by the American Enterprise Institute in the years following the publication of *To Empower People*.[1] Woodson himself helped run the project for several years. He has had more field experience than most of the rest of us.

The next three essays are a little different—more like practical summaries or reflections on what went before. Stuart Butler's essay on the appropriate principles involved in thinking about mediating structures draws lessons from the essays immediately preceding it and also begins where the two historical-philosophical essays in part one leave off. Butler attended all three seminars of the working group that planned this book, in which we listened to early drafts of the various chapters and raised questions about them. Drawing on these discussions as well as on his many years of writing about these problems, he sets forth a series of general propositions to guide newcomers to the field and to serve as a useful checklist even for veterans.

Next, Douglas Besharov points to the complexities that result from different choices of how to generate funding for mediating structures. Some of the problems that arise when funding comes directly from the state are obvious enough. But what about funding that comes indirectly from the state? And in what ways can "bottom up" funding be generated? It is all well and good to talk about mediating structures, but any long, sustained project is bound to need steady and reliable sources of funding. How and where are these to be found?

And then, so as not to allow part three to end on a completely optimistic note, I call attention to the seven different *types* of questions that arose during our seminars and now again in the chapters here presented. The concept of mediating structures is not a simple one, since mediating structures come in all shapes, sizes, and forms, and their relations to the larger society, and even to government, are many and various. This concept is closely related to three others powerful in the world of ideas today: the principle of subsidiarity, the law of association, and civil society. We do not want to leave this subject without calling attention to many different lines of thought yet to be investigated.

Finally, in part four, Peter Berger and Richard Neuhaus, to whom we are all indebted for inspiring so much stimulating work, respond to the earlier essays. They find that they have not had to change their minds very much, if at all, on the basic propositions they presented in 1977. But they have come to see how much more complex is the process of realizing the ideal they there set forth. And they make some astute comments on current changes in the intellectual climate. The present moment seems to be much more receptive to their new approach to social problems than was the intellectual climate of 1977. Now is an auspicious moment to revisit the "first principles" they then set forth and to bring a new generation into the argument.

Those of us involved in this project think that this new approach to social policy is as potent and, in its way, as socially promising as the ideas in the possession of Franklin D. Roosevelt and his closest circle in 1932, when the New Deal began its fifty-year unfolding. We think that the political party that best makes mediating structures the North Star of a new bipartisan agenda will dominate practical politics for the next fifty years. Those who cherish the preeminence of the little platoons and associative networks of civil society over the bureaucratic state are more deeply rooted in the original ground and genius of the American experiment.

There are bound to be deficiencies in such an approach. But it is never wise to let the perfect become the enemy of the good. It is also unwise to trust the state excessively. And it is usually prudent to place your bet on human liberty. Men are not angels, and on this earth we will never create an earthly paradise. What the approach to public policy through mediating structures promises is not paradise, but only a significant and more humane alternative to the tangle of pathologies our nation now experiences. We hope these essays stimulate others to carry this approach forward, with wisdom and to great effect, especially for the poor.

PART ONE

The War of Ideas

2

A New Civic Life

Michael S. Joyce and William A. Schambra

Recent events seem to have confirmed the exhaustion of the grand political project for America that was outlined in 1909 by Herbert Croly's *The Promise of American Life*, elevated to electoral hegemony by Franklin Roosevelt and the New Deal, and pursued with single-minded resolve throughout most of this century by progressive liberal theorists and politicians alike. That project might be summarized as the effort to construct within America's borders a great national community, which would summon Americans away from selfish interests and parochial allegiances toward a commitment to an overarching national purpose. How this project came to be, how it came to collapse, and how civic life in America might be rebuilt on an older understanding of local community and citizenship is an urgent topic.

The Traditional Civic Order

The progressive project of national community emerged at the turn of the century, in response to what appeared to be dramatic and permanent changes in the way Americans had traditionally conducted their everyday civic life.

Before the modern age, American life had been organized around what historian Robert Wiebe described as "island communities."[1] As this apt phrase suggests, civic life was characterized by

11

both its self-containment and its cohesiveness. Individuals were closely bound one to another by strong families, tightly knit neighborhoods, and active voluntary and fraternal groups. Through these small, local, "human-scale" associations, Americans not only achieved a sense of belonging and connectedness but also tackled the full range of social and human problems that today have largely become the province of government. As sociologist Robert Nisbet noted, "The social problems of birth and death, courtship and marriage, employment and unemployment, infirmity and old age were met, however inadequately at times, through the associated means of these social groups" (or "intermediate associations," as he called them in *The Quest for Community*).[2] Citizens thus had a significant say—and *knew* they had a significant say—in the most important decisions affecting their own everyday lives. What we today call public policy was not a manufacture of government but a lived daily experience.

Thus, a citizen's churches and voluntary groups reflected and reinforced his moral and spiritual values and imparted them to his children, surrounding him with a familiar, self-contained, breathable moral atmosphere. Voluntary social welfare associations ministered to the community's vulnerable according to tenets of compassion and charity. A citizen's schools, whether publicly or privately funded, enshrined those values, and were run in accordance with them, with extensive citizen involvement and supervision. Critical public decisions were made in township meetings, ward conclaves, or other small, face-to-face gatherings in which the individual's voice was as important as his vote. The most important decisions about citizens' lives were made not by faceless others in some distant state or national capital; they were made by and among the citizens themselves, in gatherings of neighbors and acquaintances.

This, of course, is the America celebrated and immortalized in Alexis de Tocqueville's *Democracy in America*. "Americans of all ages, all stations in life, and all types of dispositions are forever forming associations," he noted, because this was how virtually every significant public problem was solved.[3] The weak central state, he noted, was not just an accident of history but the design of the Founding Fathers, who understood that the civic commitments and communal skills critical to a free society could be developed only by sustained interaction within small, intimate, decentralized settings.

"The lawgivers of America did not suppose that a general representation of the whole nation would suffice," he noted. "They thought
it also right to give each part of the land its own political life so that
there should be an infinite number of occasions for the citizens to
act together and so that every day they should feel that they depended on one another."

The Rise of the National Community Idea

In the view of the progressives who emerged at the beginning of the
twentieth century, however—theorists like Walter Lippmann, John
Dewey, and, of course, Herbert Croly and public figures like Theodore
Roosevelt and (to some extent) Woodrow Wilson—this decentralized, self-governing, and vital way of life was doomed. In their view,
the irresistible forces of modernity were beginning to sweep away
the boundaries that historically had preserved the island communities. Modern means of communication—telegraph, telephone, the
high-speed press—had breached the small town's borders with a
relentless barrage of information about the larger world, ending its
isolation. Technology had given rise to vast corporate giants whose
operations reached far beyond the jurisdictions of any single state
or city. Great cities had sprung up, populated by aggregates of isolated, disconnected individuals rather than by tightly knit neighbors. Immigration added millions more people from threateningly
alien cultures to these already forbidding metropolises. Political
control all too often passed out of the hands of town meetings, into
the grasp of what were described as corrupt, boss-driven political
machines. Citizenly duty seemed to have been lost in the stampede
for wealth, a stampede that was legitimated by new doctrines of
emancipated individualism.

In short, the forces of modernity had precipitated a crisis of
community in America: the small town and its civic virtues had
been shattered. As Lippmann described it, modernity had forever
and permanently "upset the old life of the prairies [and] destroyed
village loyalties."[4] While it was pointless, in the progressives' view,
to try to preserve or restore the ethos of the small town (that had
been the failed Populist response), it was now possible to move to a
new and higher form of community: the national community.

The essential instrument of this new and higher form would
be an active national government. In Croly's famous formulation,

the Jeffersonian values of "community of feeling and . . . ease of communication" could now be established within the nation as a whole, using the Hamiltonian instrument of a vigorous central government. As Dewey described the progressive project, the "Great Society created by steam and electricity" would have to be converted into the "Great Community."[5]

The central government, for instance, could tame through regulatory measures those great and disruptive concentrations of private wealth, the corporations, thereby turning them into "express economic agents of the whole community," as Croly put it. The government would also become "expressly responsible for an improved distribution of wealth" and would begin to alleviate, through the progressive income tax and social welfare programs, the inequalities of wealth that might imperil the sense of national oneness. A vigorous program of "Americanization" would serve to integrate diverse immigrant populations into a single, coherent people. "Scientific management" and other new developments in the social sciences held out the promise that enlightened, bureaucratic administration could order and direct toward public purposes the chaotic popular masses. (As sociologist Charles Horton Cooley put it, the era demanded "a comprehensive 'scientific management' of mankind, to the end of better personal opportunity and social function in every possible line.")[6]

Behind these specific developments and programs, however, lay a larger moral purpose: the creation of a genuine national community that could evoke from the American people a self-denying devotion to the "national idea," a far-flung community of millions in which citizens nonetheless would be linked tightly by bonds of compassion, fellow feeling, and neighborliness. In Croly's words, there would be a "subordination of the individual to the demand of a dominant and constructive national purpose." A citizen would begin to "think first of the State and next of himself." Again, "individuals of all kinds will find their most edifying individual opportunities in serving their country." Indeed, America would come to be bound together by a "religion of human brotherhood," which "can be realized only through the loving-kindness which individuals feel . . . particularly toward their fellow-countrymen."

The catalyst of the national community, the articulator of the "national purpose," in the progressive view, was to be the president—the galvanizing, unifying voice of all the American people.

The president's is the "only national voice in affairs," Woodrow Wilson argued. He alone can unite and inspire the people by combining their many views into one coherent whole: "The voices of the nation unite in his understanding in a single meaning and reveal to him a single vision, so that he can speak . . . the common meaning of the common voice." From the "bully pulpit" of the executive office, the president would summon from the American people the self-sacrifice, public-spiritedness, and compassion that the national community requires.

This vision of national community reached its apotheosis in World War I. Suddenly, the progressives discovered the awesome capacity of war—the capacity to nurture public-spiritedness and national oneness. Dewey would speak appreciatively afterward of the "social possibilities of war." Lippmann noted approvingly that "the war has given Americans a new instinct for order, purpose, and discipline" and had served to "draw Americans out of their local, group, and ethnic loyalties into a greater American citizenship." Liberalism would never forget the lessons of 1917–1918. Henceforth, in times of peace, it would search diligently for the "moral equivalent of war," a kind of war that would energize the national community without the actual spilling of blood.

The National Community and the Eclipse of Citizenship

At the level of the citizen, this new philosophy of national community began to introduce dramatic changes in the way everyday civic life was experienced. Whereas before, public affairs were well within the grasp of the average citizen, easily comprehended and managed by ordinary folk wisdom and common sense, now public affairs had allegedly been so complicated by modernity that, according to the progressive elites, the average citizen could no longer hope to understand or manage them. Now it was necessary, in E. A. Howe's phrase from *Wisconsin: An Experiment in Democracy*, to "call in the expert."[7]

Thus, Dewey urged broad public education in the social sciences so that citizens would learn, in Timothy Kaufman-Osborn's formulation, "the radical insufficiency of the maxims of everyday conduct." They would learn as well that "the roots of most problematic situations do not lie within the jurisdiction of the locality and hence that their commonsense analyses of those situations are unreliable."[8] The good citizen would now accept his "inescapable dependence upon those trained in the expert methods of the social sciences" and graciously back out of public affairs in deference to the experts who alone knew how to manage the complexity of modern public life. As city management advocate Henry Bruere put it, "Citizens of larger cities must frankly recognize the need for professional service in behalf of citizen interests. . . . Even efficient private citizens will evidence their efficiency by supporting constructive efforts for governmental betterment."

For the progressive elites, "governmental betterment" meant reforms in governing systems that all but ensured deference to the new professionals by structurally elevating public affairs out of the average citizen's reach. Historian Samuel Hayes points out that decentralized, localized ward and precinct systems of representation, which had "enabled local and particularistic interests to dominate" and had ensured that elected officials "spoke for. . . those aspects of community life which mattered most" to the average citizen, now gave way to at-large, citywide systems of voting and representation, which handed over governance to corporate and professional elites possessed of an enlarged, scientific, rational view of governance.[9]

As Hayes suggests, structural revisions such as the short ballot, initiatives, referendums, recalls, and the city manager system that familiarly present themselves as prodemocratic, antimachine reforms might in fact be better understood as methods to subvert and undermine the private civic associations through which common citizens had previously expressed themselves, in the effort to ensure enlightened elite rule. In Hayes's formulation, the earlier, decentralized system "involved wide latitude for the expression of grass-roots impulses and their involvement in the political process." The progressive vision, by contrast, "grew out of the rationalization of life which came with science and technology, in which decisions arose from expert analysis and flowed from fewer and smaller centers outward to the rest of society."

The triumph of progressive structural reform would mean, in essence, that citizen involvement in public affairs was reduced from active, intense, face-to-face problem solving on a daily basis to passively casting a lonely, solitary ballot once in a great while for a handful of offices. That ballot would be aggregated with vast numbers of other solitary votes into a mandate for an elite corps of professional experts, who would now conduct the real business of public life.

Similar "reforms" ensured that local schools were removed from the hands of everyday citizens organized around religious or ethnic values. As Sol Cohen suggests, the decentralized, neighborhood-based management of the New York school system came under assault in the 1890s by reformers who were particularly anxious to drive religious expression and teachings out of the schools: "The reformers' battle cry, 'Take the school out of politics,' not only meant take the schools out of the hands of Tammany Hall, it also meant take the schools out of the hands of the Roman Catholic Church."[10] Joel Spring notes that "declining local control of the schools" was paralleled by "the increasing differentiation, specialization, and centralization of school administration," all of which "contributed to a decrease in lay influence on the schools."[11]

The anxiety about the presence of religious values in public schools arose, of course, from the conviction that traditional, sectarian religion was but a benighted, retrograde system of myths that must be purged from common consciousness to establish the undisputed hegemony of the social sciences. Indeed, many of the progressives understood the new sciences and their seeming capacity to reorder society into a coherent and orderly whole to be an evolution from or substitute for religion, a realization of a secular Kingdom on Earth; one may recall here Croly's formulation, a "religion of human brotherhood." J. David Hoeveler directs us to progressive University of Wisconsin president John Bascom's view that "a theology which seeks the regeneration of society in ignorance of social laws is doomed to failure" and his consequent conviction that a government possessed of such laws was "a surrogate for the churches and voluntary societies."[12]

Bascom's evident hostility toward churches, voluntary societies, and other private civic institutions completes the picture of progressivism's understanding of public life. Experts needed to replace civic and voluntary social programs not only because those civil institutions represented backward, unsophisticated citizens hopelessly encumbered by retrograde values but also because only the social sciences understood how to manipulate the powerful, subtle forces of modern society that in fact had produced social problems in the first place. The model for social policy was now a corps of professional social scientists organized into rational bureaucratic structures ministering to passive "clients," who were understood to be the blameless and helpless victims of those modern forces. This

would replace what Bascom dismissed as a "rambling halting vol-
untaryism"—bumbling, amateurish, parochial, unenlightened voluntary charities, which mean spiritedly insisted on holding those
victims to a standard of personal moral responsibility and expected
them somehow to exert themselves on their own behalf.[13]

It should be apparent by now that progressive liberalism was
not altogether forthright about its motives for moving toward a
national community through bureaucratization, rationalization, centralization, and the centripetal moral impulse of the national idea.
On the one hand, progressives insisted with sociologist Robert Park
that "the old forms of social control represented by the family, the
neighborhood, and the local community have been undermined and
greatly diminished" simply as the inevitable and irresistible result
of the forces of modernity.[14] On the other hand, as Robert Nisbet
maintains, there is no mistaking the fact that the progressives were
actively hostile to such intermediate associations and worked hard
to destroy them by shifting their functions and authority upward to
the national state and its elite corps of experts.

The national community project thus was not somehow thrust
upon reluctant progressive reformers by modern trends. It was in
fact the culmination of human progress, in their view, the finest
and most complete form of political and social organization imagin-
able, fully meriting every conscious effort to bring it to reality—
even if that meant euthanizing civic institutions that might not, in
fact, be quite on their deathbeds.

The implications of the progressive program were not lost on
prescient observers at the time. Presidential candidate Woodrow
Wilson sounded the alarm: "What I fear. . . is a government of experts," he noted in his 1912 Labor Day Address in Buffalo. "God
forbid that in a democratic country we should resign the task and
give the government over to experts. What are we if we are to be
[scientifically] taken care of by a small number of gentlemen who
are the only men who understand the job? Because if we don't understand the job, then we are not a free people."

Before the decade was out, of course, Wilson would himself
succumb to the charms of the progressive project and the "social
possibilities of war." After a hiatus in the 1920s, this project would
be brought to political power by Franklin D. Roosevelt's New Deal
and then pursued relentlessly throughout the rest of the century
by a succession of powerful, energetic progressive presidents.

The Reign of the Progressive Community

Indeed, every great liberal president of the twentieth century following Wilson made the cultivation of the national community the
central goal of his administration, expanding the power and reach
of the national government and calling on Americans to put aside
self-interest and local allegiances on behalf of the national idea (often invoking the phrase *moral equivalent of war*). The explosion of
government power during the New Deal, for instance, proceeded
from Roosevelt's call in his first inaugural address for Americans to
"move as a trained and loyal army willing to sacrifice for the good of
a common discipline." We must be "ready and willing to submit our
lives and property to such discipline," he insisted, and pledge that
"larger purposes will bind upon us all as a sacred obligation with a
unity of duty hitherto evoked only in times of armed strife."

The historian Samuel Beer notes that historians and economists have debated endlessly the intentions and effects of the vast
outpouring of government programs during the New Deal. But "in
creating among Americans the expectation that the federal government could and should deal with the great economic questions and
that the nation could and should bear the consequent burdens, the
achievement of the New Deal was close to revolutionary." (Beer
brings an insider's perspective: as a young speechwriter for
Roosevelt, he notes, "I vividly recall our preoccupation with per-
suading people to look to Washington for the solution of problems.")[15]

Similarly, we remember John F. Kennedy above all for his stir-
ring call to Americans to put aside self-interest on behalf of national purpose: "Ask not what your county can do for you—ask what
you can do for your country." Concrete accomplishments aside,
Kennedy promised to make us feel as a nation that we were together, united, "moving again." "These are times that appeal to every citizen's sense of sacrifice and self-discipline," he announced
during the campaign of 1960. "They call out to every citizen to weigh
his rights and comforts against the common good."

Liberalism's national community project reached its zenith in
Lyndon Johnson's aptly named Great Society (though it would have
been better named the Great Community). Again, there was the
familiar explosion of federal government activity, justified by an
equally familiar rhetoric: "I see a day ahead with a united nation,
divided neither by class nor by section nor by color, knowing no

South or North, no East or West, but just one great America, free of malice and free of hate, and loving thy neighbor as thyself."America, he insisted, must "turn unity of interest into unity of purpose, and unity of goals into unity in the Great Society."

The centerpiece of the Great Society was, of course, the "war on poverty"—selected with the careful progressive eye for moral equivalents. "War," Johnson explained, "evokes cooperation...[and a] sense of brotherhood and unity." The "military image" of the war on poverty, he argued, would "rally the nation" and "sound a call to arms which will stir people. . . to lend their talents to a massive effort to eradicate the evil."

In this case, the people chiefly stirred to lend their talents turned out to be vast cadres of social scientists, armed with the very latest theories about the insidious social forces that "created" poverty and an endless array of federal programs designed to manipulate those forces on behalf of their putative clients, poverty's passive, helpless victims. Indeed, the Great Society probably came as close as any other effort in the twentieth century to capturing progressivism's ideal: public policy securely in the hands of an elite cadre of professionals, dispensing programs through vast, gleaming, rational bureaucracies—a domestic version of Johnson's "best and brightest," who were busily designing another kind of war elsewhere.

New Doubts about the National Community

Beginning in the early 1960s, however, there were ominous rumblings beneath the apparently smoothly humming federal edifice. Powerful intellectual and political movements, spanning the ethnic and ideological spectrum, began to suggest that the national community was not quite so coherent or compelling as progressivism had hoped it would be. Indeed—despite six decades of progressive warfare against "parochial" civil institutions—there appeared once again a yearning for the intimate, face-to-face, participatory community to be found in small groups, family, neighborhood, church, and ethnic and voluntary associations.

The New Left, for instance, insisted that the Great Society was, despite its claims, radically anticommunitarian, characterized by (in the Port Huron Statement's formulation) "loneliness, estrangement, [and] isolation." This was inevitable in a society governed by what they now described as a massive, distant, alienating bureaucracy, linked closely with giant business concerns in that unholy alliance the New Left came to call "corporate liberalism." As an alternative, the New Left offered "participatory democracy." A society organized according to that principle would devolve major political and economic decision making to small, tightly knit local groups, within which people would "share in the social decisions determining the quality and direction of their lives." (The communitarian strand of radical thought would ultimately be overwhelmed, however, by its companion doctrine of personal liberation and uninhibited self-expression, which would go on to play its own havoc with our civic institutions and values.)

The rejection of the national community and the impulse toward smaller, more intimate communities also characterized the Black Power movement of the 1960s and 1970s and the subsequent flowering of similar movements centered on ethnic identity and community control that it inspired. According to Stokely Carmichael and Charles Hamilton in *Black Power*, Blacks should begin to "recognize the need to assert their own definitions, to reclaim their history, their culture; to create their own sense of community and togetherness." Local social institutions such as the schools and police should not be run by white liberals downtown, but by Blacks in the neighborhood: "We must begin to think of the black community as a base of organization to control institutions in that community." By celebrating Black culture and morality in their own public places, a "growing sense of community" at the neighborhood level would be further encouraged.[16]

So powerful were these new doctrines that Senator Robert Kennedy seized upon them for his electoral challenge to Johnson's Great Society. He argued in *To Seek a Newer World* that the nation's slums could be transformed only through "new community institutions that local residents control, and through which they can express their wishes." He called for a "decentralization of some municipal functions and some aspects of government into smaller units, no matter what the race or economic status of the governed."[17] This would, he noted, move us "toward [Jefferson's] vision of participating democracy," an objective that had otherwise become "increasingly difficult in the face of the giant organizations and massive bureaucracies of the age."

Perhaps the most politically potent expression of dissatisfaction with the national community in the 1960s and 1970s, however, came from the opposite end of the political spectrum, from lower-middle-class blue-collar neighborhoods, usually connected to the older industrial cities of the North and East, usually heavily ethnic (of Southern and Eastern European origin), Democratic, and Catholic. As they saw it, the national government seemed to have launched a massive assault—through cold, bureaucratic edict or equally cold judicial fiat—against the traditional prerogatives of locality and neighborhood to define and preserve their own ways of life. Suddenly, they could neither pray in their local schools, nor indeed count on sending their own children *to* the local school because of compulsory busing, nor ban from their communities forms of expression or sexual conduct that they considered offensive, nor define the conditions under which abortion might be proper, nor even enforce the most rudimentary forms of civil order under the police power.

Describing the deeper impulses behind the white ethnic revolt, Michael Novak in *The Rise of the Unmeltable Ethnics* suggested that ethnics had historically been the primary victims of progressive liberalism's effort to eradicate particularist allegiances on behalf of one vast homogenized, rationalized, bureaucratized national community. Now they had made a dramatic and forceful "turn toward the organic networks of communal life. . . family, ethnic groups, and voluntary associations in primary groups."

Meanwhile, a similar discontent was afflicting the evangelical South and West. The initial (but not the final) expression of this discontent came, of course, from George Wallace, who insisted that people were "fed up with strutting pseudo-intellectuals lording over them. . . telling them they have not got sense enough to run their own schools and hospitals and domestic institutions."[18] Consequently, Wallace explained, there had been a "backlash against the theoreticians and bureaucrats in national government who are trying to solve problems that ought to be solved at the local level." His answer to this was "States Rights and local government and territorial democracy."[19]

The Political Eclipse of National Community

Beneath the variety of intellectual currents of revolt during the 1960s lay this central truth: progressive liberalism's intention to eradicate "parochial" loyalties on behalf of the great national com-

munity had failed miserably. That failure became ever more con-
spicuous during the 1970s and 1980s. The nation's political land-
scape reshaped itself to accommodate the groups that had been
roused to an angry political revolt over the assault on their "organic
networks."

The often overlooked fact is that after 1964, *no one* would again
win the presidency by boasting about building a Great Society, a
great national community, in America. *No one* would again call
proudly and forthrightly for a shift of power to Washington and
away from the local organic networks. Indeed, every president from
1968 to the present has placed at the center of his agenda the *de-
nunciation* of centralized, bureaucratic government, along with
promises to slash its size and power and to reinvigorate states, small
communities, and civil society's intermediate associations.

Thus, President Richard Nixon complained that "a third of a
century of centralizing power and responsibility in Washington has
produced a bureaucratic monstrosity, cumbersome, unresponsive,
ineffective." He proposed a New Federalism in which "power, funds,
and responsibility will flow from Washington to the State and to the
people," through block grants and revenue sharing. During the presidential campaign of 1972—even after he had presided over four
years of dramatically *expanding* government—Nixon would nonetheless insist that the "central question" of that election was: "Do
we want to turn more power over to bureaucrats in Washington. . .
or do we want to return more power to the people and to their State
and local governments, so that people can decide what is best for
themselves?" Similarly, President Gerald Ford characterized his programs as an effort to "return power from the banks of the Potomac
to the people in their communities."

During this period, Republican presidential hegemony would
be interrupted but once, by an "outsider" Democrat who asserted
that the Republicans had, rhetoric notwithstanding, permitted the
federal government to become too large and inefficient. What was
needed, Jimmy Carter declared, was an engineer's savvy to trim
government back to size. Thus, his schemes for reorganizing government, zero-based budgeting, and sunset provisions were aimed
at proving government could "serve basic needs without proliferat-
ing wasteful, bloated bureaucracies." Cultivating his image as a man
steeped in the moral and religious traditions of a small Southern
town, Carter promised a new emphasis on local community: "The

only way we will ever put the government back in its place is to restore the families and neighborhoods to their proper places," because they can "succeed in solving problems where governments will always fail."

Carter, of course, eventually drifted away from his pledge to reduce government and restore the prerogatives of families and neighborhoods. Faced by shrinking popularity, he resorted to what almost amounts to a self-caricature of liberalism's favorite ploy: discovering another moral equivalent of war. In his now infamous "malaise" speech, Carter suggested that "we are the generation that will win the war on the energy problem and in that process rebuild the unity and confidence of America" (as if shivering in an underheated home, remembering to turn out the lights, or sitting in endless queues at gas stations would somehow restore our faith in the central government and sense of national oneness).

Americans were not particularly pleased to be told that they suffered from "malaise," nor were they up for a "war" that simply masked yet another expansion of federal power, in this case the nationalization of energy supplies. Thus was Carter replaced by this century's most consistent and eloquent critic of federal power and spokesman for reinvigoration of local community. Ronald Reagan promised an end to the state of affairs in which "thousands of towns and neighborhoods have seen their peace disturbed by bureaucrats and social planners through busing, questionable education programs, and attacks on family unity." He called instead for "an end to giantism, for a return to the human scale. . . the scale of the local fraternal lodge, the church organization, the block club, the farm bureau" and pursued that concept through budget reductions, block grants, a program of private sector initiatives, and a (new) New Federalism. His successor, George Bush, in turn followed Reagan in explicitly rejecting liberalism's project of national community, proclaiming instead a vision of "a nation *of* communities, of thousands of ethnic, religious, social, business, labor union, neighborhood, regional, and other organizations, all of them varied, voluntary, and unique," which would stand as a "thousand points of light" in America's struggle to solve social problems.

Republican ascendancy in the 1990s was terminated when President Bush not only failed to reduce government but actually acquiesced in its expansion through significant tax hikes. His victorious opponent—like Carter, draping himself in the traditional val-

ues of a small Southern town, albeit called Hope rather than Plains—
swore that he had gotten the message about his party's traditional
allegiance to big government.

Proclaiming himself a "New Democrat" by way of shorthand
for this political epiphany, Bill Clinton pledged to end welfare as we
know it, to get tough on crime, and to "reinvent" government (which
insiders understood to mean "revive" but which the public could be
counted on to mistake for "reduce"). Publicly, he would raise questions
about reliance on big government and suggest a return to the "organic networks": as he noted, "our problems go way beyond the reach
of government. They're rooted in the loss of values, in the disap-
pearance of work and the breakdown of families and communities."
Problems will be solved, he continued, only when "all of us are willing to join churches and other good citizens…who are saving kids,
adopting schools, making streets safer."

What explains an erosion of the idea of national community so
severe that even the Democratic party itself now hesitates to speak
up for it? In part, it must be noted, the moral momentum of national community is extremely difficult to sustain. The project strains
to create, artificially and at the level of the nation, a mutuality and
oneness that appear readily and naturally only at the level of the
family or local community. This transfer may be possible in times of
crisis, when the threat to the nation is sufficiently obvious that people
do, indeed, feel obliged to pull together as one.

The United States has experienced its share of such crises since
1929—the Great Depression, World War II, the cold war—and liberalism used them to maximum effect, to construct an ever more
powerful central government. The extraordinary community-
mindedness of national crisis is extremely demanding, however, and
therefore difficult to sustain, especially when real crises are not
available and liberal presidents must turn to moral equivalents.
But war on poverty (to say nothing of a "war on the energy problem") is but a pallid substitute for the real thing. Today, with the
end of a long and exhausting cold war, Americans seem distinctly
unwilling to rally around the "national idea."

With the moral foundations of the liberal project thus eroding,
its programmatic superstructure—a massive, centralized federal
government—is left in a peculiarly exposed and precarious position. No longer understood to be the instrument of high national
purpose, the federal government comes to be seen instead as a dis-

tant, alienating, bureaucratic monstrosity. In the wake of this development, it was inevitable that the American people would return to the idea of community that finds expression in small participatory groups such as family, neighborhood, and ethnic and voluntary associations—an idea far more natural and easier to sustain.

That such a return is profoundly difficult and complicated after eight decades of liberalism's campaign of civil eradication is only to be expected. The consistent and ever-intensifying message from our most "sophisticated" cultural and political institutions over that period was that such local civic institutions are at best sources of amusement, at worst hopeless backwaters of reaction, racism, and religious superstition and zealotry. In light of this unremitting barrage of cultural denigration, it is all the more remarkable that the American people nonetheless continued throughout the past quarter-century to express themselves politically *against* the national community and *for* local, organic networks.

Perhaps the only other political phenomenon evidencing itself as consistently over the past twenty-five years has been the steadfast failure of our national leaders to respond substantively to it, solemn quadrennial promises to the contrary notwithstanding. Indeed, the dramatic and ever-increasing gap between what the public *demands* and what federal officials actually *deliver* once in power has spawned whole analytic industries in political science, economics, and talk show punditry. Government programs have mysteriously acquired "lives of their own"; "runaway" entitlement spending has somehow passed beyond the realm of human control; a swarm of invisible but omnipotent special interest groups are choking the life out of democracy; Congress's committee structure is hopelessly fragmented and can no longer discipline itself; government branches in different partisan hands collapse helplessly into "gridlock," "stalemate," "divided government"; we even hear today the patronizing psychopolitical hypothesis that the American people are fickle and self-contradictory, and do not *really*, in their heart of hearts, *want* to reduce government.

Again and again, for twenty-five years, our political elites have carefully and cleverly explained to the American people that, even if they no longer believed in big government or its higher purposes, big government is nonetheless here to stay. And again and again, for twenty-five years, the American people have trudged patiently, wearily, but—one clearly senses—ever more angrily to the polls to vote against it.

Viewed in this larger perspective, it is now perhaps easier to understand the tsunami of 1994. For the seventh time in a quarter-century, the American people in 1992 had elected the presidential candidate who had persuaded them that *he* was the most sincere about reversing the growth of government (all three candidates had earnestly made that claim). And for the seventh time, early deeds such as proposing government absorption of the health care industry quickly gave the lie to words and told the American people that, once again, they had been had.

The 1994 election was no infantile tantrum at the polls, as has been suggested by some analysts. It was, rather, the culmination of twenty-five years of frustration, twenty-five years of promises made and broken. By 1994, the American people simply could not bring themselves, in the words of the ancient injunction, to "forgive, not seven times, but seventy times seven."

The Resuscitation of Civil Society

Understanding the full dimensions of the growing ill humor of the American electorate evident in 1994 is essential, if we are to begin to restore faith in American institutions. Michael Sandel suggests that "the election was haunted by the fear that we are losing control of the forces that govern our lives, that the moral fabric of community is unraveling around us, and that our political institutions are unable to respond."[20]

As Sandel implies, Americans have remained relatively untroubled about the abstruse macroproblems our governing elites would like them to worry about (because they seem to call on scientific, government-managed expertise for solution)—problems like work force retraining for global competitiveness, the greenhouse effect, and long-term interest rates. Rather, Americans are worried above all about the unraveling of the orderly, coherent, authoritative moral community they were once able to build around themselves within their own strong, local, civic institutions. They are deeply troubled by the sense that they are not safe from random violence in *this* house or *this* neighborhood; that they cannot send their children safely down *this* street to the local school; that they can no longer rely on *this* school to teach their children both rigorous basic academics and sound moral values in tune with *their* deepest spiritual and ethical commitments. And they have long since stopped trusting the experts who assure them that crime rates are really falling, or that children are really better off without pedagogy about right and wrong, or that disruptively immoral behavior is really just an alternative lifestyle.

As we have seen, our major governing institutions and elites have not only done little to prevent the erosion of local civic community—indeed, this has been their primary intention for much of this century. Our elites have spent eight decades explaining to the American people that modern circumstances are far too complex for them to hope to govern themselves—far better to shift public decision making upward to sophisticated, rational elites who have scientifically mastered those circumstances. In this view, the local civic institutions to which the people cling are just distractions from the grand national idea.

Further contributing to the erosion of those institutions has been the elite's ethic of unfettered self-expression, which they gladly inherited from the New Left. Beneath its dizzying variety of moral, political, and sexual manifestations, this ethic is at its heart nothing more than an in-your-face repudiation of the everyday, bourgeois moral code that the American people once counted on to preserve the immediate civic order. As Robert Nisbet intimated, the embrace of the doctrine of hyperliberated individualism has added a potent weapon to progressivism's arsenal in its campaign to sap the power and authority of intermediate associations.

If the message of 1994 and of every presidential election since 1968 is that the American people have utterly lost faith in the project of national community and the elites who would construct it, then perhaps we would be wise at last to heed the other half of the past quarter-century's message. For the American people have also been patiently and consistently telling us that they wish to get about the business of reconstructing the local moral and political institutions of civil society and rebuilding the social order they ensure.

They understand that only strengthened local government and revitalized intermediate institutions—families, neighborhoods, churches, schools, and ethnic and voluntary associations—will permit them to reestablish fundamental decency and basic civil order within their immediate surroundings. They wish to make the most important decisions about their own lives for and among themselves, so that once again things are seen to be "under control." In short, the American people will no longer settle for occasionally casting a ballot for one or another set of elites. They insist on becoming, once again, genuine self-governing citizens.

The restoration of civil society will require nothing less than a determined, long-term effort to reverse the gravitation of power and authority upward to the national government and to send that authority back to local government and civil institutions. Some of the proposed structural reforms put before the public by the 104th Congress during 1995—term limits, the line-item veto, the balanced-budget amendment, and so forth—might be useful first steps in that direction. But they are only first steps, the damage-control measures that must be taken while a vastly more significant positive agenda is pursued in tandem.

That positive agenda is once again to empower civic institutions, local governments, families, and citizens to make the public decisions and carry out the public tasks that really count. This includes especially the most significant decisions and tasks within the realm of social policy—the economic, social, educational, and moral sustenance of the youngest, oldest, poorest, and most vulnerable. As Peter Berger and Richard John Neuhaus suggested, we must make mediating structures the primary agents of social welfare.

3

Community without Politics— A British View

David G. Green

The first edition of *To Empower People* was written mainly with America in mind, and my brief for this new edition is to offer a European (mainly British) view. The original essay began with an apparent paradox: that there was, on the one hand, a demand for more services from the welfare state and, on the other, animosity toward big government. The authors went on to argue that, instead of looking to the government to provide additional welfare services, Americans should put their trust in mediating structures.

This essay has two aims. First, it tries to describe a way of looking at European political philosophy that explains the place of intermediate associations in a free society. Second, it describes British experience of welfare before the welfare state with the intention of explaining how, well into the twentieth century, a tradition of private welfare was successfully maintained. It depended on the deliberate cultivation of a sense of public responsibility that was independent of politics. It relied, in other words, on a sense of "community without politics." Its renewal is one of the urgent tasks of the age.

But first I will offer an interpretation of the historical development of the modern European state. According to the philosopher Michael Oakeshott, since medieval times European states have been

torn between two contradictory methods of association: "civil association" and "enterprise association." Each type is based on different assumptions about two other fundamental questions: the
character of the people composing the association (human nature)
and the tasks and limits of government. Together, the principle of
association, the conception of human nature, and the attitude to the
role of government constitute what Oakeshott calls the "three inseparables."[1] All political philosophies make assumptions about those
three elements, whether explicitly or not. The challenge is to keep
all three in mind as we reflect on the respective spheres of government and people.

An "enterprise association" is composed of persons united in
pursuit of a common interest or objective. A nation might comprise
many such enterprise associations, including business corporations,
but here I am concerned with nation-states of this type. In its pure
form such a nation has one single purpose, and the task of government is to manage the pursuit of this goal and to direct individuals
as appropriate.

In a nation of "civil associates" people are related to one another, not because they share a concrete goal but because they ac-
knowledge the authority of the laws and morals under which they
live.[2] The task of the state under a civil association is to play its part
in maintaining the laws and applying them and to supply services
such as defense, which of necessity must be financed from taxation.
The government is limited and under the law. Its task is not to manage people but to create the conditions in which people can freely
associate for self-management.

A civil association is not a mere collectivity of disparate individuals. There is a strong bond of solidarity but one very different
from the unity typical of an enterprise association. In a civil association the sense of solidarity of the people, as well as the legitimacy
of the government, derives from the shared sense that the social
system gives everyone a chance to do the best he can in his self-
chosen sphere of life. And it depends on the sense that we are all
pulling our weight to uphold the personal virtues on which a free
society relies.

The sense of solidarity in an enterprise association, however,
derives from the belief that each person is part of a single grand
scheme, perhaps to modernize or develop the nation's resources or
to mold human character in a new direction. In an enterprise asso-

ciation, people are seen as role players contributing to a wider scheme. They may be conceived as requiring decisions to be made for them, and they are assumed to need direction, because of their inability or indisposition to choose.

In a society of civil associates, the individual is seen not as a role player under management but as a thinking person capable of creativity and judgment, bearing personal responsibility, and guided by beliefs, choices, sentiments, or habits. Individuals so conceived are the carriers of a moral compass: in short, each is a person with a character rather than an individual with a role.[3] This freedom is seen as a pleasure, not a burden. It is valued for its own sake, not only because it may lead to wanted outcomes. Indeed, it is taken to be what gives man dignity.[4]

The terms *civil association* and *enterprise association* do not necessarily describe particular societies but represent the polar extremes of a continuum on which societies can be placed. Such societies may fluctuate between the extremes, and while civil association represents the most desirable type in most conditions, in national emergencies like war it may be necessary for a free society to transform itself into an enterprise association.

Oakeshott's focus on the three inseparables helps us to avoid the caricatures of a free society that are always readily to hand. It is not a nightwatchman state. The powers of government are limited, but its task of maintaining the conditions that allow liberty is positive and demanding. It also calls for leaders capable of putting their own interests last in the search for those impartial rules that protect us all.

People are not seen as mere "economic men," rationally calculating their way through life, but as moral agents facing challenges, making judgments, and doing their bit. And the society is not to be understood either as a collection of separate individuals, each going his own way, or as a community united under leadership in pursuit of a common purpose. There is real unity—not, however, the mystical bond favored by philosophers inclined to glorify "the state" and whose ideas provided a rationale for twentieth-century fascism and communism. It is a bond based on practical duties, on the one hand, to conduct an inner struggle to be a better person and to raise children who owe a similar allegiance and, on the other, to give of our own time to help the less fortunate so that no one suffers alone. Moreover, these duties are taught and upheld as an alternative to the coercion that inevitably accompanies state intervention.

The Family

All civilizations depend on agreement about moral principles; yet during the past thirty years or so, even the most sure-footed experts in their field have become as unsteady on their feet as toddlers when they turn their minds to morals. In the rush to avoid being seen as killjoys, puritans, authoritarians, or prigs, or fearful that we may be accused of "blaming the victim," we have lost the capacity for calm and measured debate about moral issues. And this weakness is in part the result of the state of disrepair into which our mediating structures have fallen. They are important not only as potential providers of nonstate welfare but also as builders of character and upholders of the virtues indispensable to liberty.

How should we understand man's moral nature? Adam Smith's view has as much relevance today as in the eighteenth century. He saw the human condition as a struggle for improvement, both materially and morally, and he believed that God had implanted in man an emotion that, if properly harnessed through human institutions, tended to increase mutual consideration and diminish selfishness. Smith called this emotion "sympathy," and the opening sentence of *The Theory of Moral Sentiments* describes it thus:

> How selfish soever man may be supposed, there are evidently some principles in his nature, which interest him in the fortune of others, and render their happiness necessary to him, though he derives nothing from it, except the pleasure of seeing it.[5]

Nature, said Smith, endowed man with "an original desire to please, and an original aversion to offend his brethren" and "taught him to feel pleasure in their favourable, and pain in their unfavourable regard." But morality was not merely a matter of feeling good when we please others and bad when we do not. There were two "tribunals," said Smith. The first was, indeed, based on the plain desire for "actual praise, and in the aversion to actual blame." But the jurisdiction of the second—the "man within"—was founded on the desire, not for mere praise, but for "praiseworthiness, and in the aversion to blameworthiness."[6] Praiseworthiness was not a purely personal standard of morality, but the yardstick of what Smith called the "impartial spectator." It was what a sociologist might call "internalized values" or a theologian, conscience.

Aristotle had taken a similar view. None of the moral virtues are natural, says Aristotle. They are engendered in us: "Neither *by* nor *contrary to* nature; we are constituted by nature to receive them, but their full development in us is due to habit."[7] We acquire virtues by exercising them. People become builders by building, musicians by playing instruments, and "just by performing just acts, temperate by performing temperate ones, brave by performing brave ones."[8] So, he continues, "it is a matter of no little importance what sort of habits we form from the earliest age—it makes a vast difference."[9] Good habits dispose us to act in just ways, hence, Aristotle says, the importance of having been trained "from infancy to feel joy and grief at the right things: true education is precisely this."[10]

Such a morality demands a lot of the family, for it is in the family that children spend time with adults who are sufficiently committed to them to devote long hours to molding their character. For Adam Smith the family was fundamental. If it failed, little could be done to make up for lost ground, and the key to success was regular close contact. In modern terms, Smith was an advocate of quantity time over quality time, and he urged parents not to send their children away to boarding schools because, by living at home, "respect for you must always impose a very useful restraint upon their conduct; and respect for them may frequently impose no useless restraint upon your own."[11]

But not all moral systems are consistent with liberty. There is a sense in which a morality, though not coercive, might be suffocating. The type of practical or habit-based morality consistent with civil association is one that is evolving and tolerant of defiance. There is a tension at its heart that is, up to a point, welcomed. Yes, there should be a clear view about right and wrong, so that children can be given unequivocal guidance. But the moral system must be able to change with circumstances and avoid rigidity. A good measure of the tolerance and adaptability of a moral system is its attitude to eccentrics. Moral eccentricity, says Oakeshott, is of value to a society whose morality is based on good habits. The attitude of society toward an eccentric "is necessarily ambivalent." He is "admired but not copied, reverenced but not followed, welcomed but ostracized."[12] In asserting the neglected importance of mediating structures, and especially the family, we also need to renew our understanding of the tolerant, adaptive moral system that leaves room for the eccentric. A morality for freedom should offer a clear yardstick against which we can judge ourselves, but there must be tolerance of defiance and eccentricity as well as tolerance of the critics of defiance.

What should we make of the oft-voiced claim that it is authoritarian to call for a moral renewal? The idea underlying the censure of the self-styled anti-authoritarians is that man is naturally good and that, consequently, we need to clear the way for our innate goodness to shine through by sweeping away corrupting institutions and guilt-ridden moral codes. But as Aristotle and Adam Smith understood, nature prepares us for morality, but it does not supply us with a finished product. We are social creatures, and the moral code under which we inevitably live is a shared responsibility. But this recognition does not imply control. There can be responsibility without control; authority without commands; community without politics; and respect for our common heritage without central direction. Writers like Lord Acton valued liberty precisely because it set conscience over the authorities. Liberty, he said, is "the reign of conscience." It consists "in the preservation of an inner sphere exempt from state power."[13] But while we can hope for morality without authoritarianism, there can be no functioning morality without mediating structures such as the family.

What can be done? If it is desirable to restore family life, how should it be accomplished? And what role should government play in upholding the family? The libertarian interested in abstractions would argue that it should do nothing: government should be neutral between lifestyle choices. But to maintain such a stance is not as easy as it seems, so long as the government accepts responsibility for maintaining the safety net below which no one should fall. The payment of benefits has two types of effect. It has an obvious incentive effect, much studied by economists, but also what James Q. Wilson calls a tutelary effect. That is, the very act of paying or not paying a benefit sends a signal of approval or disapproval. If the state sends cash to unmarried mothers to raise their own children rather than sending a social worker to encourage them to have their babies adopted by couples able to give them a better chance, the message is unambiguous. Public policies send moral messages in addition to producing incentive effects.

This means that neutrality is not an option. Unless it is to withdraw altogether from welfare, the state cannot help sending moral messages. The only question is, What should the message be? Adam Smith is again instructive. He saw the danger of stipulating duties but concluded that the family was so essential and the consequences of failure so serious that the state must use its powers to uphold the traditional family. The law should for the most part prohibit injury, but, Smith thought, it can and should go further:

> The laws of all civilized nations oblige parents to maintain their children, and children to maintain their parents, and impose upon men many other duties of beneficence. The civil magistrate is entrusted with the power not only of preserving the public peace by restraining injustice, but of promoting the prosperity of the commonwealth, by establishing good discipline, and by discouraging every sort of vice and impropriety; he may prescribe rules, therefore, which not only prohibit mutual injuries among fellow-citizens, but command mutual good offices to a certain degree.[14]

Smith saw that it was potentially dangerous for laws to require the fulfillment of duties of benevolence:

> Of all the duties of a lawgiver, however, this, perhaps, is that which it requires the greatest delicacy and reserve to execute with propriety and judgement. To neglect it altogether exposes the commonwealth to many gross disorders and shocking enormities, and to push it too far is destructive of all liberty, security, and justice.[15]

Law, for instance, was important in encouraging the best in family life. If divorce was too easy, he argued, it tended to undermine trust between the couple, because both were "continually in fear of being dismissed by the other party."[16] He accepted that divorce law could be too strict but thought it better that the knot was "too strait" than too loose.[17] The law of inheritance was also important. Illegitimate children, for instance, ought not to inherit because if they were allowed to do so fathers might take correspondingly less interest in their legitimate offspring.[18] The law had also played an important role in making the relationship between men and women in marriage more equal, a development of which he approved.

Adam Smith saw clearly the importance of the family in a free society, and he saw that the law must uphold the duty of parents to care for their own children and discourage divorce even at the risk of being too strict. Legal reforms and benefit revisions cannot alone restore the tradition of marriage as a commitment, but because of the tutelary as well as the incentive effects of public policies we cannot hope for change unless the government plays its part.

Rebuilding Community without Politics

How could assistance of the poor, provision against contingencies like ill health, and education be restored to civil society?

Poverty and Philanthropy. The modern doctrine of welfare rights seems at first sight to be based on respect: our common humanity, so the argument goes, demands that we all enjoy equal rights. But in truth the demand for rights removes the relationship between giver and receiver from the moral domain. It de-moralizes the relationship. We should aim, therefore, to base a policy of assisting the less fortunate, not on "rights," which are demands that other people be compelled to render assistance, but on duties, which reach within us all for our better nature.

The ideal to aim for is mutual respect between giver and receiver: no presumption of superiority by the giver and no doffing of caps by the receiver. This spirit is captured by an incident in Dickens's *Hard Times* when Stephen Blackpool, an honest and hard-working power-loom weaver, is unfairly sacked by the factory owner, Josiah Bounderby. His plight is desperate, for he has no money and no chance of other work in the locality without a reference from Bounderby. He faces a long and arduous journey by foot in search of employment. Bounderby's wife, who believes her husband has been unjust, offers Stephen some money to see him through the hard times ahead. He takes only £2, a much smaller sum than she offered because, he says, he knows he can pay that much back.[19] In other words, despite his dire predicament, he will not allow the relationship to be one-sided and will accept only a loan. Mutual respect between giver and receiver has been maintained.

The giving of help is undoubtedly difficult to accomplish in the right spirit, and during the past century great effort was expended to discover and encourage the right approach. The charities of that time issued their employees and volunteers with guidelines or manuals, some of which have been described in an excellent study of philanthropy by F. K. Prochaska:

> Remember, it is a "privilege" not a "right" to enter the poor man's cottage. Be sympathetic, not patronizing. Be a friend, not a relieving lady. Avoid giving money. Do not promote a spirit of dependence. Distinguish cases of real misery from those of fictitious distress. Avoid favouritism. Be an expert on domestic management. Quote the Scriptures. Avoid religious controversy. Encourage school attendance. Avoid politics. "Show that almsgiving is not merely the duty of the rich, but also the privilege of the poor." Be regular in your visits.[20]

There is no perfection in the handling of such complex relationships, but the Victorians tried and tried again to get it right. It is time for a renewal of their struggle.

To rebuild philanthropic effort will require at least two things. Certainly, government should create the space for the reemergence of a public-but-not-political domain, which means that it must withdraw. But also, without waiting for the government, champions of liberty should establish voluntary associations for assisting the less fortunate and run them in a spirit compatible with liberty. They should aim to meet two conditions: no government money should be taken; and beneficiaries should be treated, not purely as victims of circumstance, but with the respect due to men and women of character capable of self-improvement and of, once more, making a positive contribution. The guiding principle is that practical help is superior to mere almsgiving, whether by charity or by the state. Real caring means time and trouble.

Ideally, an organization should be founded to coordinate voluntary associations conforming to this code and to encourage the new spirit among other associations. It should try to build a movement of those who take pride in ensuring that vital tasks are undertaken without resort to government. During the eighteenth and nineteenth centuries, this was the prevailing ethos of the British friendly societies and charities. For instance, arguing against proposals for a compulsory state pension scheme in 1882, a spokesman for the 600,000-strong Ancient Order of Foresters friendly society pointed out that thrift had succeeded in considerably reducing the number of paupers. The increased facilities for thrift "afforded to the British Workman by his own peculiar organisations," friendly societies and trade unions, had done much during the previous thirty years to reduce pauperism, he said. They could look forward to the time when pauperism would be reduced to those suffering from "insanity and contagion" and pointed with pride to the reduction in pauperism since 1849. In that year, paupers had comprised 6.2 percent of the population of England; in 1859, 4.4 percent; in 1869, 4.7 percent; and in 1879, only 3.0 percent.[21] In 1892 the figure was still lower at 2.6 percent.

Today, in sharp contrast, the British government regularly puts out press releases declaring with pride that the take-up rate for this or that benefit has increased. Perhaps we may hope that in time international organizations like the Organization for Economic Co-operation and Development will publish figures showing the proportion of each country's population that is *in*dependent. Very few people today take personal pride in assuming responsibility for the direct resolution of social problems; yet for much of the history of Britain and America free citizens were only too keen to establish committees or organizations to tackle the issues of the day. This activism is still a part of the Western make-up, but today it is more likely to lead to demands that the government, that is, somebody else, take action. The churches were once central to encouraging private philanthropy, but today they too are more likely to demand action by the state. They are also likely to define the good citizen as the one who demands state measures with the greatest vehemence, a doctrine that is the very opposite of the spirit of philanthropy consistent with liberty. Their doctrine is doubly pernicious because, on one hand, it denies personal responsibility and, on the other, it dresses up demands for political action as altruism when they are no such thing.

Business corporations can play a part by reorganizing their corporate giving to concentrate resources on voluntary associations that rely 100 percent on private finance and by refusing to support voluntary associations that are little more than official offshoots of the government and that in all likelihood see their role as pioneering provision for new "needs" with the intention of demanding that such needs be met universally out of taxes in due course.

Government should encourage the process by withdrawing tax-exempt status from organizations that benefit from government grants. They should have a choice between government grants or tax breaks. They can have one or the other, but not both. Governments cannot do much of a positive nature, but they could learn the nineteenth-century lesson that the huge flowering of charity took place against the background of the poor law. The state provided the bare minimum, and charitable effort was directed toward helping people to remain free from the poor law. It is, therefore, possible to maintain an official minimum without discouraging private philanthropy. But the government must not be tempted to expand welfare beyond the minimum, because for every step it takes above that minimum it displaces voluntary effort.

The practical problem is that, if the government abruptly withdrew, there would undoubtedly be some hardship. It is vital, therefore, to build up an autonomous voluntary sector first to offer a satisfactory answer to the inevitable question, Who will provide welfare if the government withdraws? There need to be off-the-shelf solutions ready and waiting.

Mutual Aid and Voluntary Hospitals. Of greater numerical importance than charities in Britain were the friendly societies, mutual aid associations whose purpose was to foster independence by allowing people to band together. A family could be independent if the breadwinner had work, but there was no margin to provide for self-support if the breadwinner fell ill or died or was unable to find a job. Consequently, mutual aid associations emerged to allow members to spread the risk. Societies provided all the services that enabled people to be self-supporting:

- earnings when the breadwinner was ill or injured
- support for the widow and orphans when the breadwinner died
- support in old age, although the usual attitude was to keep working as long as possible with the fallback of sick pay
- traveling in search of work (including internationally)
- medical care when ill. (Usually doctors were paid a capitation fee in return for free care. But the societies also organized medical institutes where service was provided by salaried medical officers.)

In Britain, when the government introduced compulsory social insurance for 12 million persons under the 1911 National Insurance Act, some 9.5 million were already providing the same services for themselves through voluntary insurance associations, chiefly the friendly societies. Friendly society membership far exceeded that of the other characteristic organizations of the working classes, the trade unions and the cooperative societies. In 1910, the last full year before the 1911 act, there were 6.6 million members of registered friendly societies, quite apart from those in unregistered societies. There were only 2.5 million members of registered trade unions and 2.5 million members of cooperative societies.[22] The rate of growth of the friendly societies over the preceding thirty years had been rapid and was accelerating. In 1877, registered membership had been 2.8 million. Ten years later it was 3.6 million, increasing at an average of 90,000 a year. In 1897 membership had reached 4.8 million, having increased on average by 120,000 a year. And by 1910 the figure had reached 6.6 million, having increased at an annual average rate since 1897 of 140,000.[23]

How can the government create the space in which such organizations can emerge again? During the nineteenth and twentieth centuries the attitude of the state toward the friendly societies altered radically, thereby helping us to compare the effects of different legal frameworks. There were three main periods: before 1834, the friendly societies were subject to paternalistic supervision by the justices of the peace; between the 1834 Friendly Societies Act and the 1911 National Insurance Act, classical liberalism was the general rule; and from 1911, paternalism made its return. The heyday of the societies was the period from 1834 to 1911 when the government confined itself to maintaining a framework of law, and to requiring disclosure of information to the public, but without interfering in the internal management of societies.

The lesson is that voluntary associations should be truly independent of the embrace of the state, free to set premiums and benefits, to decide whether to function on commercial, mutual, or philanthropic lines, and to govern their own affairs under the law of the land. When the government imposed national insurance in 1911, the societies were forced to become "approved societies" under the act. A full account of the results is given in *Reinventing Civil Society*,[24] but the essential facts were these. Premiums were no longer voluntary contributions but taxes, and benefits no longer the "manly right" of the member's earlier thrift but stipulated by statute. The innovation and diversity that had been the norm before 1911 were suppressed, and the competition and consumer choice typical of the nineteenth century were eradicated at the behest of organized medicine, which demanded increased pay for doctors and reduced accountability to the consumer as the price of its participation in national insurance.

If the ideal is a society of civil associates, then the role of the state should be confined to maintaining the laws that protect everyone's liberty, and it should resist the temptation to steer human energies in the direction desired by the ruling party or faction. Here then is a different principle from the one defended earlier for the family. The state should leave room for voluntary associations, but it should not dictate how they should be managed or the form they take. The family is different. When two people create new human life, choosing to take no responsibility for their child is not an option that can be exercised without high costs for both the child and others. To defend any lifestyle choice out of a desire to be consistent—that is, out of a wish to follow an abstract principle to the bitter end—is very far from abstract in its effects. Consequently, the state can properly embody the obligations of parents in law.

Hospitals. Hospitals were nationalized in Britain in 1948. Until that time, the voluntary hospitals provided the backbone of the acute hospital service. Nearly 60 percent of patients requiring acute care were admitted to voluntary hospitals in 1936.[25] They also provided the overwhelming majority of teaching hospitals.

To what extent did the voluntary hospitals rely on private finance, and how rapidly had private funding developed? The best contemporary source of information is a report by Political and Economic Planning on *The British Health Services*, published in 1937. It was written by socialists who wanted a state hospital service but found it necessary to report that in 1935, while unemployment was still high, the voluntary hospitals had an annual surplus income of over £1,000,000. The authors can give only grudging praise, conceding that "despite the depression," the majority of voluntary hospitals have "temporarily" overcome their financial difficulties.[26]

Voluntary hospitals originally provided free care, but when concern grew that it was degrading to rely on charity, movements evolved to allow people to pay. Hospital contributory schemes (a kind of prepaid insurance) developed rapidly during the second half of the nineteenth century to allow people in lower-income groups to make regular contributions entitling them, without further inquiry into their means, to receive free hospital treatment for themselves and their dependents. By 1936 at least 10 million persons were covered.[27]

In addition, for those not in contributory schemes hospital almoners were appointed to discuss with individuals how much they could afford to pay. These developments gradually reduced the reliance of voluntary hospitals on charitable donations for running costs. In 1891 charitable donations comprised 52 percent of running costs. The proportion had fallen to 26 percent in 1938. Charitable donations were being replaced by patients' payments either in the form of modest fees, assessed according to income, or through contributory schemes. Donations and bequests were used for capital investment, demand for which was ever growing as the pace of medical advance accelerated.

This record of the voluntary hospitals has a double significance. They had been providing not only an improving service for decades by the time they were nationalized but also a focal point for people of good will in the locality. Individuals could help as hospital visitors, or as fund raisers if that was where their talent lay, or in providing "extras" like books for patients to read, or running a voluntary canteen. The hospitals were outlets for all those human decencies, great and small, that make life worthwhile. Under nationalization the tendency was for all services to be provided by paid staff, guided less by altruism and more by their trade union rule book.

Hospitals are among the most important mediating structures because of their ability to harness local good will, which is in part because they work with the grain of human nature: it is in everyone's interest to have a good local hospital. Hospital ownership in America is far more diverse than in Britain, where hospitals remain nationalized and unable to fulfill their potential as mediating structures.

Schools. Schools, like hospitals, have a special significance. They not only pass on accumulated knowledge of past generations to children but also teach moral virtues. In addition, they too are a focal point for parents and local residents to give of their time and energy for the good of others. Again, fund-raising talent and organizing skills will be useful, but there is also a niche for parents to assist the teachers in the classroom. Extra help, for instance, allows young children to spend more time reading aloud to an adult. Altogether these qualities rank schools among the foremost mediating structures, and we cannot hope to mend the fabric of civil society without restoring schools to their proper place.

Critics of state monopoly in schooling have traditionally argued for a voucher scheme. Their reasoning is that education standards are too low because education is provided by local public sector monopolies, which are insufficiently concerned with parents' presumed preferences for high standards. The remedy is to put the consumer in the driving seat by allocating parents a voucher sufficient in value to buy education in a school of their choice for each of their children. Schools that attract parental support will flourish; and those that are unresponsive to parents' preferences will fail to attract pupils and will find it necessary to mend their ways or close. Some authors add to the basic idea an element of equalization: children in low-income neighborhoods, for instance, would be given vouchers with a higher cash value to make up for the poverty of their home background.

The chief risk of a voucher scheme is that governments will abuse their power to define which schools are entitled to receive public funds. Such power could be used to create entry barriers, thus maintaining an effective public sector monopoly. One possible answer is to lay down only minimal conditions, covering relatively few matters such as health and safety and minimum standards for teacher certification, so that the registration of schools under the scheme could not become a significant barrier to the entry of new schools. Teachers, for instance, should not be required to undergo lengthy training. A bachelor's degree or its equivalent should be sufficient, combined with initial training within schools.

A second approach would be to bar the government from laying down conditions and to leave the responsibility to parents. For instance, a rule might be enforced giving a school able to attract fifty or more pupils a right to receive voucher finance. A cross between the two approaches might be better still. For instance, the government could maintain a register of schools that met defined requirements and a register of those that did not. Vouchers would be payable to registered and unregistered schools, thus leaving it to parents to decide whether they valued registration as an indication of merit or not. Private schools should, of course, be included.

Both the traditional voucher and the egalitarian variant focus on the demand side, with supporters putting their faith in the enfranchisement of parents as the mechanism that will stimulate change on the supply side. It is doubtful, however, whether demand-side changes will be sufficient to break the power of entrenched public sector monopolies. Schools should have total control of admissions, school numbers, governing structure, teacher tenure, training, and salaries. They should set their own fees and not be accountable for their performance to any political authority, but only to parents. It is very difficult to see how such independence could be accomplished without radical supply-side deregulation.

It is now well established that the key to the successful functioning of any market is the possibility that new entrants will attract customers from existing providers. Without this discipline, established suppliers too easily settle down to a quiet life. For this reason, it would be desirable for neither central government nor local authorities to have the power to run schools and to relinquish control of existing schools. This could be accomplished by means of a phased hand over to independent educational trusts.

All told, this combination of measures would break public sector monopoly, allow new schools to emerge spontaneously, and offer the best chance of achieving the ultimate purpose of reviving the ethos of teaching as a vocation and reactivating dormant parental responsibility.

A further possibility would be to go one step further on the demand side by introducing personal payment rather than vouchers. There are two main advantages compared with voucher finance. First, payment more fully restores parental responsibility and thereby strengthens the family. The children's awareness that their parents are paying for their education creates a strong bond helping to unite the generations. Second, there would be less reason for governments to interfere because they would no longer have the excuse that they were exercising caution in spending public funds, a special difficulty in America because of the constitutional separation of church and state.

A scheme for parental payment has been proposed by Sir Roger Douglas, the former finance minister of New Zealand.[28] He reserves vouchers for people receiving welfare benefits or guaranteed minimum family income (the equivalent of America's earned income tax credit). They are to be given a voucher sufficient to buy education in a local school. The remaining majority are expected to pay fees. To ensure they have sufficient cash, however, income tax is to be cut. A high tax threshold is to be set (NZ$32,000 for a man, wife, and child), which, compared with the existing tax system, leaves families some NZ$8,000 better off, easily enough to pay for education, which is valued at about NZ$3,500 for primary school and NZ$4,500 for a secondary. The chief difficulty of schemes involving payment is that they may deter people on benefits from moving into paid work. This deterrent is reduced by tapering away benefits at fifty cents on the dollar so that there is always some financial gain from work. Moreover, anyone working whose income falls below the NZ$32,000 threshold, and who is not receiving a social security benefit, will receive $1 for every $3 shortfall. Someone earning, say, NZ$22,000, would receive NZ$3,333.

But under his scheme, will people on low pay, even with the general and education-specific tax credits, have enough to pay school fees? This question, however, is based on the false assumption that earnings are fixed, whereas if people are short of cash because they have school fees that must be paid, the parents have a reason to increase their earnings by working overtime, taking a second job, or acquiring skills in the hope of commanding a higher wage. People are not wholly the victims of circumstance. As J. S. Mill wrote:

> The business of life is an essential part of the practical education of a people; without which, book and school instruction, though most necessary and salutary, does not suffice to qualify them for conduct, and for the adaptation of means to ends. Instruction is only one of the desiderata of mental improvement; another, almost as indispensable, is a vigourous exercise of the active energies; labour, contrivance, judgment, self-control: and the natural stimulus to these is the difficulties of life.[29]

Under Douglas's scheme, there is ample help, but he does not try to eliminate all the "difficulties of life." And with good reason, for as Mill warned:

> A people among whom there is no habit of spontaneous action for a collective interest—who look habitually to their government to command or prompt them in all matters of joint concern—who expect to have everything done for them, except what can be made an affair of mere habit and routine—have their faculties only half developed.

Such a system, said Mill, "embodies the idea of despotism, by arming with intellectual superiority as an additional weapon those who already have the legal power."[30]

Another potential difficulty is that if schools are free to set their fees, a school in a given locality could put itself beyond the reach of some poorer parents. This difficulty is overcome under a voucher scheme so long as schools are required to take children from the locality at the voucher value. Under a fee-paying system, it is more difficult. If existing government schools are transferred to the control of educational trusts, however, then a condition of the trust deed could be that children from a defined catchment area must be accepted at the value of the maximum tax credit ($3,500 for primary and $4,500 for secondary schooling). This requirement would preserve neighborhood links, guarantee access for all, and secure the advantages of payment rather than vouchers.

School trusts could also be empowered to establish scholarship funds. The payment of scholarships to able pupils, and bursaries to parents who get into temporary difficulty, is already common practice and could easily be extended, providing another outlet for private philanthropy. No doubt other potential drawbacks can be identified, but after many decades of the welfare state we have surely learned that political promises to remove the "difficulties of life" are not without cost.

Conclusions

It is important not to think of freedom as the absence of obstacles to our desires, a view that might be called the "get-out-of-my-face" theory of freedom. The free way of life that has emerged slowly in Europe since the Middle Ages, with many setbacks on the way, is not only about removing obstacles. It has three related elements. It is based on a real sense of solidarity that unites people in upholding the virtues on which freedom rests. It assigns to government the high honor of maintaining the laws and preconditions for free association, not least by protecting a domain of initiative and creativity for each person. And it rests on a view of human nature that sees people, not as the "rank and file" under orders, or semichildren in need of paternalistic but benevolent guidance, but rather as capable of exercising personal responsibility. This view of individual potential is both a factual claim about the principles of social organization most consistent with human nature and an ideal to aim for. In a free society so conceived, the mediating structures of family, voluntary association, church, and neighborhood are indispensable.

Let J. S. Mill have the last word:

> The only security against political slavery is the check maintained over governors by the diffusion of intelligence, activity and public spirit among the governed . . . . It is. . . of supreme importance that all classes of the community . . . should have much to do for themselves; that as great a demand should be made upon their intelligence and virtue as it is in any respect equal to; that the government should. . . encourage them, to manage as many as possible of their joint concerns by voluntary co-operation.[31]

PART TWO

Implementing the Idea in Politics

4

Mediating Structures, 1977–1995

James P. Pinkerton

Ironically, the most poetic and memorable evocation of mediating structures in our time came from a politician not known for his oratorical skills, one who had publicly dismissed the "vision thing." Yet George Bush painted the following picture of the good society in his acceptance speech to the Republican Convention in 1988. He spoke of "the idea of the community" as

> a beautiful word with a big meaning, though liberal Democrats have an odd view of it. They see community as a limited cluster of interest groups, locked in odd conformity. In this view the country waits passive while Washington sets the rules.
>
> But that's not what community means—not to me.
>
> For we are a nation of communities, of thousands and tens of thousands of ethnic, religious, social, business, labor union, neighborhood, regional and other organizations, all of them varied, voluntary, and unique.
>
> This is America: the Knights of Columbus, the Grange, Hadassah, the Disabled American Veterans, the Order of Ahepa, the Business and Professional Women of America, the union hall, the Bible study group, LULAC, Holy Name—a brilliant diversity spread like stars, like a thousand points of light in a broad and peaceful sky.

Peggy Noonan, who provided the poetry, recalls that the initial impetus for the speech came from Bush himself: "The Vice President told me: 'It's local organization, it's the local thing that can make the most immediate and obvious difference in people's lives. It's local people that do these things.'" [1] Noonan synthesized Bush's gut feelings, together with the communitarian writings of William Gavin, Michael Novak, and William Schambra, to create the rich political imagery that broadened Bush's appeal in the November election.

So ideas have consequences. But how much consequence? Looking back at the domestic record of the last four presidents, one can see that all failed to grasp the potential for a new humane and human-scaled politics. Bush was notable because he so spectacularly raised expectations, encouraging voters in 1988 to believe that he could develop a kinder, gentler, nonbureaucratic activism—all without raising taxes. As it happened, he achieved none of those goals; the consequence for him came in 1992.

The 1994 elections were a further reminder that politicians linked to a deteriorating status quo will also face severe electoral consequences. The greatest impact of *To Empower People* will be felt in the future: incumbents who made their careers by centralizing and disempowering will likely find that their political survival requires a strategic repositioning; challengers, always looking for a new platform upon which they can ride into office, will find that the antimainframe wind of history is at their back.

To Empower People, published in the first year of the Carter administration, reflected some of the corporatist *Zeitgeist* of 1977. Peter Berger and Richard John Neuhaus viewed bureaucratic government as one of the implacable "megastructures" that towered over people as they attempted to live their lives. Defining mediating institutions as "those institutions standing between the individual in his private life and the large institutions of public life," the authors proposed an incrementalist response: "Our point is not to attack the megastructures, but to find better ways in which they can relate to the 'little platoons' in our common life."

Yet they also heard the rumbles of the larger social forces that would undermine the giantist institutions they seemed to be making peace with. Citing popular resistance to "massification," they endorsed school vouchers, which, as the National Education Association would attest, was the most subversive plan yet for overturning the current paradigm of social-service delivery. And they also noted that the decades-long decline of religious influence "has now stopped or even reversed"—this on the eve of the New Right religious boom that has so transformed American politics in the past fifteen years.

The political change we have seen in the past two decades, however, has been vastly exceeded by the change in the economy and the culture. Also in the 1970s, a continent away from the American Enterprise Institute, entrepreneurs in what would be known as Silicon Valley were plotting a materialist revolution; in 1980 Alvin Toffler, recognizing that the economic substratum was shifting, predicted that the mega-superstructure of culture and politics would soon tumble. In *The Third Wave*, he used the term *de-massification* to describe the breakup of familiar TV networks, corporate conglomerates, and political empires.

Fast-forwarding to the 1990s, America faces this challenge: how to adapt the enduring idea of mediating structures to a cyber-Schumpeterian economic reality that subverts the very idea of permanent structures? The "awkward question" in Disraeli's 1844 novel *Coningsby* was "What will you conserve?" Today, the equally difficult question is, What will be mediated?

Carter's Good Intentions

In 1976 Jimmy Carter campaigned on character; he held himself out as the embodiment of plain-spoken Plains values. He pledged "a government as good as its people"; yet for all his personal commitment to thrifty voluntarism, the good intentions of his presidency were overwhelmed by the unintended consequences of mega-structured government.

Carter pledged a new urban policy, but he failed to develop one because his administration was staffed with recycled Great Societeers who saw their mission as picking up where the 1960s left off, even as the money spigot was running dry in the new era of limits. The few creative-thinking Carterites, such as Assistant Housing Secretary Gino Baroni, were politely ignored. Baroni helped set up the National Commission on Neighborhoods, which proved to be a brief blip on the Carter administration's "brainwave-scope." The commission provided a forum for a wide array of community activists; some of their demands did not fit within acceptable "progressive" definitions. After pro-empowerment commission members noisily agitated for a rollback of the redevelopment-inhibiting Davis-

Bacon Act, the Carter administration concluded that the commission was a headache it did not need, and even the whole apparatus was back-burnered.

The Carter administration's most significant new initiative was a billion dollars' worth of neourban renewal, Urban Development Action Grants. Thus, in the name of helping grass-roots communities, the Carter administration provided enormous subsidies to such distinctly disintermediating institutions as Hyatt Hotels.

Reagan's Accommodation to Big Government

The influence of the idea of mediating structures on the next cohort of Republican thinkers is unmistakable. To Empower People included chapters entitled "neighborhood" and "family"; so did the 1980 GOP platform. In its preamble, the Republican manifesto declared, "We seek to restore the family, the neighborhood, the community and the workplace as vital alternatives in our national life to ever-expanding federal power." Yet the language of the platform owed more to the personal enthusiasm of Republican empowerers than to the future policy agenda of the GOP nominee. Thus in his speech to the Detroit convention, the new Republican nominee conjoined the similar-yet-different ideas of federalism and mediating institutions into a single sentence: "We need a rebirth of leadership at every level of government and private life as well."

As president, Ronald Reagan was no enemy of localized decision making. But because he saw his main mission as defeating the evil Soviet empire, he had to reach an accommodation with the megastructure of the U.S. government. A few Jeffersonian decentralizers, such as Martin Anderson, John McClaughry, and Douglas Bandow, sailed into the White House with the Reagan tide in 1981, but they quickly jumped ship, frustrated by the lack of interest within the administration in any sort of domestic policy beyond Stockmanite budget cutting and Bakerite deal making. Emblematic of their frustration was the bottling up of enterprise zone legislation. Enterprise zones served as the administration's all-purpose catchall "urban policy," enabling pragmatists to assert that they did, too, have a message for the cities. Yet when Ways and Means Committee Chairman Dan Rostenkowski announced he was against it, the administration, unwilling to invest real capital in changing his mind, was left with Sam Pierce steering the ship of the Department of Housing and Urban Development.

One feeble Reagan effort was the Office of Private Sector Initiatives. This could have been an effort in which the president made common cause with authentic community leaders to overcome the regulatory hindrances that the National Commission on Neighborhoods had identified. But instead, the value system of the slick-hair-and-suspenders crowd prevailed, and the PSI became a showcase for "Friends of Nancy," in which CEOs and Hollywood types could exchange business cards and air kisses as they waited in line to get their picture taken with the Gipper. Lost amid the blue-chip noblesse-obligery was the hardy self-help ethos that Berger and Neuhaus had identified as the key to successful meditating institutions.

Some will argue that Reagan was too busy fighting the good fight against communism and inflation to concern himself with the deteriorating *Gemeinschaft* on the homefront; certainly the congressional Democrats were no help. Yet the fact remains that many baleful social trends worsened during the 1980s, even as social welfare spending continued to rise. A look at William Bennett's *Index of Leading Cultural Indicators* shows that just about any indicator—crime, illegitimacy, and divorce, to name three—worsened during the 1980s. It was Bennett, not some Democratic doomsayer, who wrote just last year that "unless these exploding social pathologies are reversed, they will lead to the decline and perhaps even to the fall of the American republic."[2]

If the voters realized that threats to the American commonweal cannot be solved by a reversion to the New Deal, it became equally clear that not all social pathologies could be solved by tax cuts.

Bush's Points of Light

Although it had a fancier name, the story of the Bush administration's Points of Light program is similar to that of Reagan's Private Sector Initiatives. While Bush speechwriters could occasionally insinuate a Hayekian paean to the spontaneous order sparked by sturdy American yeopersons, the essence of the "Points" owed less to Saul Alinsky and more to Yale philanthropy. Such was the conceptual confusion that many of the Bush-honored "points of light" were government grantees. In the acid analysis of ex-Reagan aide McClaughry, "The same politicians who got government money for groups lobbied to get those groups named as points of light, which in turn credentialed them to get still more government money."

Bush did make some progress early on. A concern raised in *To Empower People*, day care, was deftly handled by a child tax credit; a rival plan to sovietize day care was thus forestalled. Yet the Bush high command drew no larger lesson from this victory; it was content to parley with power brokers at the summit of the Beltway megastructure, letting the resulting decisions trickle down upon the populace.

One loud but lonely voice crying in this intellectual desolation was Jack Kemp. In 1990 Kemp was designated to lead an empowerment task force; yet as fate would happen, within days of his appointment, Iraq invaded Kuwait, and that spelled the end of any White House interest in domestic reform. Later that year administration hierarchs snittishly banned the use of the word *empowerment*, which left the empowerment task force in something of a quandary.

Clinton's Volunteerism

Little need be said of Bill Clinton. His major domestic initiative called for the creation of a whole new health megastructure; it was rejected. One idea he did push through was AmeriCorps. But paid volunteers, many of them "volunteering" for the federal government, can only be defined as mediating institutions if HUD regional offices are also defined as Tocquevillean associations.

Conclusions

All four presidents from 1977 to 1994 tried to work with the megastructures; each in turn has had less and less success, as the great mechanism of bureaucracy continued to wind down toward entropic obsolescence. And so the time has come for a rethinking of mediating institutions. Based on a brief survey of the empowerment efforts of the last four presidents, two sets of questions come to mind:

• First, how do we mediate between individuals and megastructures when the megastructures themselves are collapsing of their own dead weight? From Moscow to Washington to Armonk, New York, executives as diverse as Mikhail Gorbachev, George Bush, and John Akers thought they could work something

out. They all failed. What will happen to those mediating structures, such as labor unions, that came into being to countervail the
giant institutions, such as Fortune 500 corporations, that are now
downsizing? Will little platoons be equally effective at protecting
people from debris falling from the commanding heights?

• Second, if the megastructures do collapse, what happens?
Can government help only by getting out of the way? Are some boats
so broken that even a rising tide will not lift them? Newt Gingrich
is careful to say that he wants to "replace" the failed welfare state,
but can the new Republican regime be relied upon to write a new
social contract as forces beyond even the 104th Congress's control
shred the old one? Spurred on by authors Gertrude Himmelfarb
and Marvin Olasky, a major revival of interest in the Victorian era has
occurred. But will ACLU-influenced Americans tolerate a nineteenth-
century level of benevolent but meddling paternalism? But can
salvific Victorian uplift occur when mainstream religion wishes to
delegate that mission to the government?

The intellectual victory has been won; after two decades of
failure with the discredited status quo, few would argue Berger and
Neuhaus's basic proposition: that mediating structures can be the
agencies of a new empowerment. The great question now is whether
such devolutionary change can come fast enough to save American
civilization from a miniaturized, globalized whirlwind.

5

The View from the White House— Individual and Community Empowerment

William A. Galston

Public debate has evolved dramatically since the publication of *To Empower People* nearly two decades ago. Although antigovernment sentiment was already growing in 1977, the case against centralized bureaucracies and in favor of mediating institutions had not yet become conventional wisdom. Today, Scandinavian social democracy is no longer regarded as the ideal toward which we are inexorably (and happily) moving. We are increasingly conscious of the costs as well as benefits of an expanding public sector—costs measured not just in dollars but in the diminished vitality of civil society. Scholars and political activists across a wide ideological spectrum agree (at least in general terms) on the need to prune and reform the national government, enhance state and local authority, reduce regulation, and reinvigorate the voluntary sector.

Government as an Instrument of Public Purpose

In the context of this new consensus, we should not lose sight of the other side of the equation. We must not replace the simple progovernment thesis of the welfare state at its peak with the anti-government antithesis that is increasingly popular today. Government is an instrument of public purpose that can be used wisely or unwisely. Properly structured government can serve as a positive force for empowerment; it can nurture mediating institutions; it can foster liberty, rightly understood.

Empowerment should be understood, I believe, as a multidimensional social possibility. Along one dimension, individuals can be empowered to make personal choices that improve their lives—choices that may (but need not) require new or stronger associational bonds with others. Along another dimension, communities can be empowered to act in ways that promote the common good as defined collectively by their members. In these cases, associational bonds are essential to the definition and pursuit of shared goods. Empowerment, then, is frequently, but not invariably, linked to mediating institutions; it may sometimes be promoted and pursued by individuals through instruments other than these institutions.

Individuals can be disempowered in many ways—by inappropriate or unlawful acts of other individuals and by intrusive measures of public authorities but also by the absence of resources needed to make effective choices and by the failure of public authorities to do what is needed to safeguard the freedom of citizens against public or private assault. Similarly, communities can be disempowered when government restricts associational autonomy or replaces communal functions—but also when it allows one kind of civil association to deprive others of basic liberties. Sometimes government disempowers when it acts; sometimes it permits disempowerment to persist when it fails to act. Because cases and circumstances make a difference, no unidimensional view of government can be adequate to the variety of problems we confront. Let me offer a few illustrative examples.

It is easy to forget that only a few decades ago, millions of our fellow citizens were denied the most elementary civic rights and social liberties by official acts of state and local authorities. When the federal government finally intervened to end these practices, the result was empowerment—the right to vote and to stand for office, to enjoy the benefits of more equal education and training, and to make use of increased opportunity to participate in the American dream. The very familiarity of this history may lead some of us to disregard it, but it helps explain why many Americans continue to view government as a source and guarantor of empowerment.

The national government can also act to protect institutions of civil society when they come under assault. In 1990, for example, a Supreme Court decision left religion exposed to interference from state and local government. Strongly backed by the Clinton administration, faith communities mobilized around the Religious Freedom Restoration Act (RFRA), which was signed into law in late 1993. RFRA establishes a very heavy burden of proof (a "compelling state interest" that government must discharge before its laws and regulations can materially impede the free exercise of religion), and it further requires government to demonstrate that it has selected the least intrusive means available for furthering its compelling interests. RFRA is already proving an effective bulwark protecting religious free exercise against interference both from local government and from federal statutes such as the bankruptcy code.

Or consider the basic institutions of the American welfare state—social security and Medicare. It is often observed that these programs reduce the fear and insecurity that would otherwise be felt by elderly Americans. But just as important is their role in expanding the range of choices available to individuals. Once, older Americans were dependent on the good will of their children or other family members; now, many older Americans can choose where to live and with whom.

I do not mean to suggest that this change is an unmixed blessing. No doubt some ties of reciprocal obligation between the generations have been weakened by the expansion of public provision. Still, many older Americans feel newly empowered, and they are exercising their choice to form new living communities and new institutions that reflect their interests and serve their needs.

For many younger Americans, empowerment comes through postsecondary education and advanced training. Here again, government has acted effectively to expand opportunity. Decades ago, the GI Bill helped returning veterans bolster their individual prospects, discharge family responsibilities, and create new communities. More recently, loans and direct grants have allowed millions of students to make their own choices concerning the type and extent of learning that will build their future.

In the course of this process, new institutions have sprung up to serve emerging needs in ways that established institutions did not. Community colleges, for example, have boomed during the past two decades, and many of them have become new centers of life in their localities. Here again, government has empowered individuals to choose for themselves in ways that affirm and strengthen community. It is the success of this model that has led leaders in both political parties to propose eliminating the ramshackle structure of federal job training programs in favor of vouchers that would go directly to individuals to be used for the kinds of training they themselves choose.

Empowering Communities

Government can help empower communities as well as individuals. The Clinton administration's "empowerment zone" legislation, for example, offers participating communities advantages such as wage credits, capital investment tax deductions, and relief from federal regulations. As a condition of eligibility, the program requires community leaders from the public, private, and nonprofit sectors to come together around a joint plan of action. Hundreds of localities devised and submitted such plans. Reports indicate that in many communities, this required process catalyzed a kind of wide dialogue that had not previously existed. Communities that failed to receive designation as full-fledged empowerment zones nonetheless regarded the process as worthwhile in its own right, as an opportunity to inventory local resources and organize them for more effective action.

The Need for Wise Government Action

I suggested earlier that while government actions can sometimes disempower individuals and communities, in other circumstances the failure of government to act can yield disempowerment. A good example is the sphere of public safety and order. As political philosophers have long noted, the basic rules of social order must be enforced against those who have failed to internalize these rules as morally binding. This is rightly regarded as the first duty of government because it is the precondition for every activity that free individuals might reasonably choose. If law enforcement is ineffective, particularly against violence and the threat of violence, decent citizens and their children lead constricted lives, the elderly cower in their homes fearing to venture forth, and normal forms of community economic activity are strangled.

The obstacles to empowerment can be internal as well as external. Addiction, dependency, and other weaknesses of character disempower individuals just as much as do the absence of material resources and social order. Poorly structured government programs can induce, or reinforce, this phenomenon of internal disempowerment. There is little doubt, for example, that well-intentioned but misguided welfare programs have exacerbated dependency and diminished the ability of many individuals to take responsibility for their own lives.

It is not clear, however, that the remedy for counterproductive welfare programs is their outright elimination. If bad incentives weaken character, then it is at least possible that better incentives can strengthen it. Aristotle suggests that good character flows from sound habits, which are produced by repeated right action that is at first externally imposed. While government cannot wholly substitute for the formative effects of strong families and sound cultural cues, legislated benefits and burdens may nonetheless induce young adults to accept responsibility for their children and to take more seriously the imperatives of self-support through productive work. And as James Q. Wilson and others have suggested, in certain extreme circumstances it may be necessary for public institutions to intervene actively in the upbringing of young children.

Shifts in Strategy of Governance

To insist, as I have, that government can contribute to the cause of individual and community empowerment is not to suggest that government as currently constituted is well designed to promote these purposes. On the contrary, much of modern government disempowers through regulation, centralization, and the displacement of civil society by public power.

Three structural shifts in current strategies of governance would help remedy this situation:

• First, regulatory micromanagement must yield to a regime in which broad public purposes are declared, and individuals and institutions are empowered to promote these purposes in ways they choose for themselves. This shift has already begun under the leadership of Vice President Al Gore's National Performance Review; it should be aggressively accelerated.

• Second, the centralizing tendencies evident since the New Deal must yield to a revitalized federalism. Here the Clinton administration has made an important beginning. More than half the states, for example, have received waivers to pursue their own welfare reform strategies. This trend should be broadened. Indeed, the longstanding presumption in favor of the national government should be reversed; national power should be exercised only in areas where local and state government do not suffice. (In coming years, this premise of governance may well be undergirded by new constitutional doctrines in areas such as the Commerce Clause and the Tenth Amendment.)

• Third, the relationship between government and the institutions of civil society must be reordered. Other contributors to this volume have made important arguments about strategies that might enable the public sector to strengthen rather than strangle the voluntary sector. In some limited circumstances, government can act directly to invigorate local groups. (I regard the Corporation for National and Community Service as a positive example of this strategy; others disagree.)

In general, however, there is reason to doubt that government can select wisely among voluntary sector claimants for public support or that these institutions would be well served by any such "topdown" strategy. Promising alternatives include vouchers and tax incentives that would allow individuals to strengthen local associations they regard as particularly effective.

As part of this general reorientation, we must rethink the grounds on which religious institutions may join forces with government to promote important public purposes—in welfare, child care, education, and many other areas besides. My own view is that many current restrictions on public sector collaboration with these institutions are warranted neither by policy considerations nor by constitutional restraints. But that is another, longer story.

PART THREE

Civil Society's Many Faces

6

Law and the Welfare State

Michael J. Horowitz

A competition for moral and operational supremacy has occurred during the past three decades between two visions of the American legal order. The hands-down winner, a "rights-regime" approach, is based on nationwide, constitutional norms that are judicially defined and administered. The alternative "conservative vision"—a term itself regarded as oxymoronic by the mass of legal scholars—is a "contract regime" whose norms are defined by affected communities and are passively enforced by the courts on the basis of community intent and consent.

To be sure, real-world choices between these two legal visions are not always stark—statutorily *legislated* rights, for example, fall between the "rights" and the "contract" poles, approaching closer to the contract regime as legislative bodies become more local. Often, too, judges construe contracts to support the rights-based outcomes they deem "just," ignoring in the process the language of laws and contracts and the intentions of the parties who wrote them. Nonetheless, the clash of rival visions has been real and passionate.

The reach of rights regimes, by their nature, extends only to public institutions; to these alone constitutional rules attach. (The Fifth and Fourteenth Amendments, the primary source of authority for rights regimes, restrict state action only.) Thus, because people of private means can establish enclaves into which the rights writs of the courts do not significantly extend, poor people obliged to rely

on public institutions are the ones most affected by rights regimes—
are indeed largely governed by their terms and processes. This outcome is consistent with the intentions of the rights revolutionaries,
for what they sought to achieve, in the name of social justice, was a
new and better world for the poor.

A central question, therefore, is whether rights regimes have
succeeded in offering more hope and dignity to poor people or in
bettering their institutions and their lives.

History of the Rights Revolution

The important opening shot of the revolution was Charles Reich's
1964 *Yale Law Journal* article, "The New Property," among the most
influential works of American legal scholarship of the century. To
Reich, the more fulfilled lives that wealthy people are able to lead
by reason of their ownership of private property could also be significantly achieved if poor people were given comparable property
interests in the public payments they received and comparable ownership rights in the public institutions they relied on. In Reich's
view, governments should be little more able to terminate the welfare benefits of poor people than to confiscate the private assets of
the wealthy. As set forth in "The New Property" and later extended
by the courts, the government's power to evict poor people from
their public housing units was thus deemed comparable to its ability to remove middle-class people from their homes. The state's ability
to regulate conduct on public streets was said to resemble closely its
limited police power to govern private conduct in the malls and the
lawns of suburban communities. Welfare payments were to be as
protected as private annuities.

A number of consequences—some intended, others not remotely
contemplated—followed from Reich's utopian notions of empowering the poor. One consequence clearly intended by Reich was to free
poor people from obligations to comply with community-based norms
as a condition of receiving public funds or gaining access to public
institutions. (In this respect, "The New Property" bore interesting
parallels to the only other American law review article that has
approached it in importance, Brandeis and Warren's 1890 *Harvard
Law Review* article, "The Right to Be Let Alone.") A gentle and caring man tormented by a painfully closeted homosexuality when he
wrote "The New Property," Reich experienced communities as of-
ten-impinging leviathans and deeply believed that community codes

of moral conduct were as restrictive on the well-being of poor people as he felt them to be in his own life. The law of property, Reich wrote, created boundaries beyond which, save in exceptional circumstances, neither neighbors nor the state could intrude. A legal order based on a property regime, he believed, could give power and dignity to poor people in much the same way it could for him.

Reich's models of the world he sought for all were taken from early English common law property cases—those, for example, involving the right to exclude state officials from the privacy of one's home and the right to build "spite fences" on one's land to the consternation of one's neighbors. In his companion 1966 *Yale Law Journal* article, "Police Questioning of Law Abiding Citizens," Reich identified his vision for the poor with the right not to be intruded upon for conduct short of criminal activity.

In defining the optimal legal order *and the Constitution* with the right to be left alone and the right to be free of neighborly and community intrusion, Reich thus became a central intellectual figure in identifying constitutional rights with what Harvard Professor Mary Ann Glendon later described in her important book, *Rights Talk,* as the theory and practice of "radical personal individualism." In doing so—and in yet another tale of the tragically unintended consequences of utopian dreaming—Reich never glimpsed the possibility that his images of preindustrial England were not remotely transferable to the mean streets of urban ghettos, where the absence of strong community institutions and the lack of strong police presence more readily translated to social chaos and depredations against the weak and vulnerable. The lyric coda with which Reich ended his "Police Questioning"—a plea for the right to enjoy the quiet peace of a countryside amble undisturbed by sudden thunder of jet noise— nicely revealed the biases and reality gaps of his asocial vision. Lost to Reich was the fact that police questioning of suspicious loiterers was viewed by many ghetto residents as a critical mode of peacemaking, not the disturbance of peace he universalized it to be for everyone on the basis of his personal and cultural experiences.

Reich also sought a second revolutionary outcome for the poor. For him, highly empowered regulatory agencies able to control rigidly such businesses as noise-making airlines went hand in hand with operational disempowerment of such local state officials as street-corner police. And in contrast to the weakened state that he preferred where the governance of *conduct* was concerned, he sought a state sufficiently powerful to redistribute hard assets from wealthy to the poor, from producers and earners to the poor—with the latter receiving their transfers on an unearned entitlement basis, solely on the strength of their status as residents of society. Writing during a period when John Kenneth Galbraith could credibly and popularly speak of an *Affluent Society* in crisis because of its excess of consumer wealth and choice, Reich sought to transform radically common-law notions of property in order to create a constitutionally based redistributionist state. Such a view was made particularly easy for Reich by his fixed-pie view of wealth as largely resulting from government property tranfers of such assets as licenses, airwave frequencies, mining rights, and homestead acreage and by his failure to distinguish between assets transfers to which value and effort needed to be added and the entitlements to permanent annuities solely based on the "status" of poverty. Reich's redistributionist vision was explicitly articulated in a third key work, his 1966 *Yale Law Journal* article, "Individual Rights and Social Welfare: The Emerging Legal Issues." In the article's most cited segment, Reich wrote as follows:

> It may be realistic today to regard welfare entitlements as more like "property" than a "gratuity." Much of the existing wealth in this country takes the form of rights that do not fall within traditional common-law concepts of property. It has been aptly noted that "society today is built around entitlement." The automobile dealer has his franchise, the doctor and lawyer their professional licenses, the worker his union membership, contract, and pension rights, the executive his contract and stock options; all are devices to aid security and independence. Many of the most important of these entitlements now flow from government. . . . Such sources of security, whether private or public, are no longer regarded as luxuries or gratuities; to the recipients they are essentials, fully deserved, and in no sense a form of charity. It is only the poor whose entitlements. . . have not been effectively enforced.

The Importance of *Goldberg*

The second critical episode in the story of the rights regime was the one that made Reich's intellectual revolution real: the landmark decision of the Supreme Court in 1970, *Goldberg v. Kelly*, regarded by William Brennan as the most important decision he had written during more than thirty years of historically influential service on the Court. To be sure, *Goldberg* did not directly establish the full-scale Reichian right of an irrevocable entitlement to welfare payments. *Goldberg* did, however, require the state to leap over such high procedural hurdles before such payments could be terminated as to create indirectly near-irrevocable entitlements. *Goldberg's* radical mandate that "pre-termination evidentiary hearings. . . [at which] welfare recipients are allowed to retain an attorney [and are] given an opportunity to confront and cross-examine witnesses. . . are indispensable" became a powerful tool for rights revolutionaries.

To read *Goldberg* today—written as it was by Justice Brennan with a characteristic candor unmasked by dense legalisms—is to sense how the earnest mistakes of the most honorable rights revolutionaries powerfully undermined the ends they sought to achieve. *Goldberg's* critical segment, a paean to welfare payments, reveals how rights regimes were premised on views of the poor as passive victims—for whom an unearned entitlement to public money was a high moral obligation of decent social orders:

> From its founding the Nation's basic commitment has been to foster the dignity and well-being of all persons within its borders. We have come to recognize that forces not within the control of the poor contribute to their poverty. This perception, against the background of our traditions, has significantly influenced the development of the contemporary public assistance system. Welfare, by meeting the basic demands of subsistence, can help bring within the reach of the poor the same opportunities that are available to others to participate meaningfully in the life of the community. At the same time, welfare guards against the societal malaise that may flow from a widespread sense of unjustified frustration and insecurity. Public assistance, then, is not mere charity, but a means to "promote the general Welfare, and secure the Blessings of Liberty to ourselves and our Posterity." The same governmental interests that counsel the provision of welfare, counsel as well its uninterrupted provision to those eligible to receive it.

The cases that followed *Goldberg* wasted little time in restricting the discretion of local public officials in a myriad of cases: they imposed high standards of legalistic proof before officials were allowed to exercise discretionary authority and subjected them to lengthy hearings both before and after they had acted.

In the *Strickland* case, school board officials were made subject to suits for personal liability for having ordered the suspension without hearing of students who had spiked a school punchbowl with liquor. Citing Reich and *Goldberg*, federal courts barred evictions from public housing in the absence of "notice, confrontation of witnesses, counsel, and a decision by an impartial decisionmaker based on evidence adduced at a hearing"—to the point that a leading case barred the rental of a "slovenly and ill-kept apartment" to new tenants even after the occupant's signed lease term had expired. Although later reversed on appeal, a public library and police department were held liable by a federal district judge for expelling a homeless person who had stared at and stalked library patrons, had repeatedly spoken to others (and himself) in loud and disruptive fashion, and had so reeked of body odor as to have caused persons to vacate all areas adjacent to him. (The appellate reversal occurred only after the plaintiff had received a $230,000 settlement, and the judge who had rendered the 1991 opinion was, in 1994, elevated to the appeals court that had reversed him.)

Papachristou v. Jacksonville and successor cases struck down as unconstitutional the vagrancy statutes that were the prime means by which police could seek the identities of street loiterers and other suspicious persons and order them to move on. Similar decisions abounded. Fred Siegel summarized the rights regime intended trade-off of public dollars for the nonenforcement of community norms:

> In the great wave of moral deregulation that began in the mid-1960s, the poor and the insane were freed from the fetters of middle-class mores. They might henceforth sleep in doorways as often as they chose. The problem of the homeless appeared, characteristically defined as persons who lacked "affordable housing."

Political Resonance

Goldberg's authoritative identification of the Constitution with rights-regime governance also powerfully altered the terms of the natiónal *political* debate; following *Goldberg,* rights-regime victories also became increasingly routine in the legislative sphere. Thus, by way of example (and as recently described by Jackson Toby), rights-regime proponents were able in the mid-1970s to block Congress from even considering the breakdowns in discipline that were then first becoming endemic in the public schools.

State testimony delivered in 1975 by American Federation of Teachers President Albert Shanker was characteristic of invariably deprecated, losing-side claims:

> I do not think anyone can argue with the simple notion that a student about to be suspended should have. . . an opportunity to [defend himself]. But viewed in terms of a pattern of court decisions, I think one must question whether in the public schools of the United States at the present time, the greater problem is that huge numbers of students are being dealt with unjustly, suspended and expelled, or whether the problem is rising crime, violence, and vandalism. . . . I would say that at this particular juncture in the history of our schools, the great danger is not that we are doing all sorts of terrible things to innocent students.
>
> I would say the greater problem is on the other side— that we do not apprehend, that we do not punish, that we do not remove those who are perpetrating these crimes. In a period where the great problem is that form of injustice, this decision places yet another burden on the teacher, on the administrator and others. Each additional burden which is placed upon them in the administration of some form of justice is going to mean that there will be less pursuit of those who are perpetrating crime.

The winning-side claim took the form of testimony offered at the same hearing by Children's Defense Fund Director Marion Wright Edelman:

> We believe that the solution to school violence does not lie in more suspensions but less, for its causes are to [be] found more on the streets where dropouts, pushouts, and suspended students. . . pass the time among delinquent gangs in arms or drug trade. I believe it lies in the lack of preparation for decent jobs or in the lack of work even

when students are trained; and in the rates of illiteracy and its attendant frustration and anger. . . .

We believe the substantive grounds for suspension must be drastically pruned and punishable offenses redefined so that only situations which pose a direct and serious threat to people or property are causes for temporary exclusion from school. . . .

We believe that school disciplinary rules, policies and procedures, and the range of punishment for breaking them, should be made available to students and parents in writing at the beginning of each school term or year....

Blacks were suspended at twice the rate of any other racial group. . . . Some may claim that higher suspension rates for black children simply reflect greater misbehavior on the part of black students—we disagree with that. We have found what black parents, children, and civil rights groups have charged for years: that there is racial discrimination and insensitivity in the use of disciplinary sanctions.

Ms. Edelman's views were classically echoed by the counsel of the Student Rights Project of the American Civil Liberties Union, whose utopian optimism led him to believe that "there will not be substantial violence and disruption where there is meaningful education." The ACLU and the Children's Defense Fund thus recommended both greater public expenditures for education and adoption of student bills of rights to protect students against the excesses of school administrators.

During the ensuing twenty years, the political system dutifully adhered to rights regime prescriptions for educational governance. While public school officials were limited in their capacity to exercise discretion over disciplinary matters, funds spent on public schools were increased by orders of magnitude. The same period has, of course, witnessed sharp deteriorations in the performance of public schools and their increasing abandonment by urban parents having the means to do so.

Transfers of Power

A further consequence of the rights revolution involved major transfers of power. What actually occurred, however, was very different from what the revolutionaries said would happen. While they intended to transfer power from haves to have-nots, the immediate, operational effect of what they did was to transfer power from local public officials to courts and lawyers.

In so doing, hubris blinded many attorney-revolutionaries to the profound gap between the law as it sounds in well-briefed, carefully crafted appellate decisions and the law as it actually applies those decisions in real-world settings. They encouraged suits to limit the discretion of community officials in exercising authority over individuals but took no account of mismatches in resources and competency between low-paid lawyers for local bureaucracies and the often zealous and single-minded attorneys and legal service groups representing disruptive community members. Legal elites propagated abstract, utopian theories of rights and justice but barely considered the traumatic effects of their lawsuits on defendants and the pressures that litigation imposed on public officials to avoid or settle cases at all cost. No account was taken of the priority-skewing dislocations imposed on public officials by lengthy depositions or the extent to which their modestly skilled lawyers would counsel settlement and inaction rather than face the risks and hard work of actual hearings. No one factored in the extent to which imperfectly trained administrative hearing examiners would decide and dismiss cases on the basis of technical applications of imperfectly understood precedents.

Thus, a critical reality was missed by those rights-revolution pioneers who did not intend due process rights to be subterfuges for stripping local officials of all ability to deal with nonperforming or disruptive persons. They wrongly saw legal hearings as instruments of individuated, calibrated justice, not the blunt weapons they actually became for street troublemakers, unruly students, drug-dealing tenants, and others who had previously been subject to the authority of local officials. Blind to the often one-sided character of legal proceedings, the rights revolution abandoned the real interests of many public school students, public housing tenants, and community members. Those struggling to climb ladders to better lives often found these ladders, unaccountably, pushed over from above.

Bureaucratizing Effects

In the end, perhaps the most destructive feature of the rights revolution was its bureaucratizing effect and the perverse incentives it created in community officials to pursue passive, indifferent, risk-averse conduct. The public school teacher who initiated, or the public school principal who ordered, or the public school board member who sanctioned the suspension of a disruptive student often quickly found himself a defendant in a lawsuit that sought not only to reverse his decision but also to make him personally liable to the student for money damages. The public housing official who sought to reduce the influence of gangs in the projects or to evict drug dealers from their apartments found himself similarly sued, constrained, and subjected to imposing time burdens. The policeman on the beat who lacked sufficient evidence to make formal arrests when confronting known crack houses and street drug bazaars, but who still cared enough to try to break them up, was converted by the rights revolution from public protector to putative malefactor.

In the face of such challenges and burdens, in the aftermath of the substitution of lawyers and judges for local leaders and officials as protectors of the poor, it is hardly surprising that leaders of local mediating structures increasingly saw the virtues of inaction as a means of defending themselves against becoming defendants. Higher salaries for public employees became a way to get even with systems that had taken away the psychic rewards that had led teachers, policemen, social workers, and others to make their career choices in the first place. Thus, the rights revolution empowered public employee unions and aided them in turning the loyalties of municipal workers parochially inward. Often, it was less the disruptive student than the demoralized teacher, less the aggressiveness of troublemakers than the enforced passivity of authorities, that led to the diminished effectiveness of local public institutions.

Irving Kristol has observed that the only "right" given to prerevolution students was to learn what teachers thought it best to teach. This quip nicely captures the lost status and correspondingly reduced commitments of teachers decades into the rights revolution.

Legal Elites

The rights revolution in the law was of course not waged or engineered by poor people; rather, it was undertaken on their alleged account by legal elites who for years effectively painted their conservative opponents as indifferent to the interests of the poor. General skepticism about the rights regime was evidenced by polls that routinely revealed a public deeply concerned with issues of discipline, order, and values, not some supposed lack of resources or rights. When President Reagan raised the issue of school discipline and treated it as worthy of serious national attention, he was denounced by elites for staging a deceptive if not racist "sideshow." Revealingly, the public gave the president broad and extraordinary support for addressing the educational issue about which it cared most.

A telling episode occurred when President Reagan met with a number of ghetto principals who had successfully transformed their public high schools into institutions with high graduation rates, high college entrance rates, and long waiting lists. At the meeting, one of the principals first thanked the president for making the discussion of student rights a legitimate topic of national debate and then went on to describe how he had reformed his school by initiating such policies as dress codes, summary suspensions of disruptive students, and tough sanctions of students who had failed to turn in homework assignments. He spoke of how "a billion dollars" given to his school when he first came would only have been "poured down the rathole." He described how some of the more disruptive students he had first disciplined had become high-performing school leaders, once conduct norms had been made firm and clear, and then told the president the secret to his success. It was, he said, an intentional violation of existing due-process principles and a studied indifference to school board regulations dealing with student rights.

To the vigorous approval of his colleagues, he stated that his success would have been "stopped cold" had either the school board, legal services lawyers, or the American Civil Liberties Union known of what he had first done. He concluded by telling the president that "everyone now knows" his school's governing rules but that no one now tried to countermand them or to sue him. "Want to know why?" he asked the president. Told yes, he offered his punch line to the accompanying applause of his fellow principals: "My community would lynch them if they tried."

Similarly, during my term as general counsel at the Office of Management and Budget, I was visited by an angry public housing official protesting cuts that were then being considered in the federal housing budget. After the official described in moving detail

the bleak nature of life in the projects—a story more fully and powerfully set forth in Alex Kotlowitz's *Wall Street Journal* coverage of
Chicago's Robert Taylor homes and in his 1991 book, *There Are No
Children Here*—I posed two options in the privacy of my office. Under
Option A, we would not only have forgone any budget cuts but would
have doubled the appropriation the official was seeking to protect.
Option B would have given the official the right to evict summarily
no more than 10 percent of his most troublesome tenants. Asked
which option he preferred, the official first signaled the extent to
which his real feelings differed from his permissible official views
by looking around my office with mock excess to make sure that we
were alone. He responded, "Are you kidding?" All he wanted, he
said, was a decent chance to run his projects, to make his own mistakes occasionally, to have the authority with which he could be
held accountable if living conditions did not improve. That such
authority seemed to the official utterly remote confirmed the triumph of the rights revolution. Its founders had clearly succeeded
in subordinating conduct-based approaches to the pursuit of public
funds. That caring community officials who struggled daily with
the consequences of poverty might have reversed those priorities
probably never even occurred to the revolutionaries.

Other examples abound of the perverse effects of the rights
revolution's mistaken weighing of the relative importance of val-
ues-conduct versus entitlement-money issues. George Kelling, James
Q. Wilson, and Nathan Glazer have cogently argued that the health
and safety of urban communities depend less on postcrime arrest
procedures than on a community's ability to curb the spread of graf-
fiti, broken windows, and sidewalk incivility. Such tone-setting conduct is a precursor of crime even when it falls short of prosecutable
actions, and it is best dealt with by making it subject to the authority and discretion of police officers—the very power that the rights
revolutionaries radically curbed. Loss of discretionary authority by
probation and parole officers similarly reduced the community's
ability to modify the conduct of convicted felons.

Asking the Wrong Questions

Would the public housing official who spoke with me have made
bad mistakes had he been granted the eviction authority he sought
and had he been largely freed from the rights regimes of courts and

hearing officers? Would some police officers have been abusive had they been regranted the authority that street police once had? Would teachers and principals have occasionally, perhaps more often than that, disciplined the wrong students? Did welfare workers officiously assert their authority when, in pre-*Goldberg* times, they had the power to be more than entitlement-based fund disbursers? Of course, local public officials have erred, at times seriously, and will at times take action on the basis of political pressures or personal animus. But to allege this and to stop there—as the rights revolutionaries did—is to be insufficiently rigorous in considering the interests of the poor and, with advocates less honest than Brennan and Reich, to be at times deliberately deceitful.

It is, for example, to miss other and larger questions. Can communities create self-correcting mechanisms that produce increasing responsiveness and improved performance on the part of their officials? Is the accountability of officials to their communities related to the real authority they are given? Aside from short-term effects, can episodic interventions of the courts offer consistent protection against local official abuse? How far removed are courts and hearing officers (and their after-the-fact proofs) from what really happens, and how well do their findings compare with the nonlegal, intuitive, on-the-spot, and informal judgments made by experienced daily observer-officials? How critical are issues of *values*—better understood, as Gertrude Himmelfarb has pointed out, as *virtues*—in contrast to the dollar-based priorities of the rights revolutionaries? For the poor and their communities, do the harms imposed by the excesses of local officials really exceed those of the regimes that foster an ethos of radical personal individualism? To what extent has the legal rights revolution been at war with communitarian virtues?

Disrespect for Law

And what, ironically, has been the revolution's impact on the rule of law itself and the public's respect for it? Former HUD general counsel and now governor of Oklahoma, Frank Keating has described a visit that he and HUD Secretary Jack Kemp paid to a public housing project. In their traditional show-and-tell presentation to the secretary, project residents described the steps they had taken to make their world safe, doing so with great pride and a seemingly keen anticipation of secretarial approval. They spoke of how they had chosen a posse of the most menacing residents who had paid late night visits to their most troublesome neighbors and had warned them to vacate their apartments immediately lest they confront dire consequences. Beamingly, the presenters told Secretary Kemp that their efforts had rapidly succeeded in ridding their project of drug dealers and like troublemakers. The secretary did his best to compliment the tenant group without endorsing the vigilante conduct of which his presenters had been so proud.

The Keating-Kemp experience and many other comparable tales of "lawless" action taken by beset ghetto community residents are paradigms of a major real-world effect of the rights revolution that has made law a means, in Daniel Patrick Moynihan's telling phrase, of "defining deviancy down." If, as is true, the rule of law is essential to civilized order and democratic life, a further, tragic irony of the rights revolution is that it has undermined respect for the law in poor communities. The applause given by hero principals in the presence of the president of the United States when one of their own expressed contempt for the rights regime's constitutional rules was thus a signal to those who would still have defended or extended them. Sadly, it had no such effect and did not cause many such defenders, with Pogo, to take a more troubled view of at least one important *cause* of problems confronted by America's poor.

Hypocrisy of Elite Revolutionaries

It was not only errors resulting from failed utopian visions that characterize the rights revolution. A more seamy side of the tale is the self-serving hypocrisy practiced by many elite revolutionaries. Thus, while the work of such early revolutionaries as Brennan and Reich may have been based on disinterested estimates of the value of "New Property" doctrines to the poor, many of their followers were profoundly hypocritical—on two separate counts:

- The value systems they linked to the Constitution reflected highly personal interests, which they pursued on their own behalf under cover of rhetoric about helping the poor.
- They abandoned the public institutions that they had made subject to judicial rules and rights and, for themselves and their families, withdrew to private institutions governed by rules and values of their own making and choice.

As to the first hypocrisy, as elites defined *their* deviancy down to slip the bonds of gray flannel suits and Victorian constraints and to participate in sexual and drug revolutions and other modes of liberation from the norms of their communities, *they* did so while secured by safety nets of family, income, and education. Elites could also drop back into the worlds they fled (or thought they could) or could merely soften the harsher conventions of their worlds (or thought they could) with a nondestructive measure of added personal freedom. At the same time, poor people in whose name they waged the rights revolution were stripped of the norms that had heretofore facilitated their climb up the social ladder and permitted their escape from poverty's prison. The "fetters of middle-class life," which elites may at times have seen as restrictions on freedom and individuality, were for the ascending poor the very means of personhood and freer lives. Similarly, while unfettered but genteel neighbors of elites may have made for interesting company, weakened enforcement of moral norms often abandoned the poor to the destructive conduct of less benign and distinctly unfettered neighbors.

As to the second hypocrisy, here defenders of the rights revolution increasingly practiced golden-rule principles in reverse—doing unto others what they would not have dreamed of doing unto themselves. Elites who took pride in subjecting community officials to legal constraints and processes—who effectively substituted lawyers and judges for such officials as final arbiters of community conduct—lived in communities in which they and their designated officials, not the courts, drew boundary lines. Thus, while residents of public housing projects were "gifted" by elites with a legal system that sharply inhibited their capacity to evict drug-dealing neighbors, elites achieved relatively summary evictions of *their* neighbors for playing the piano too loudly. Accordingly, public housing tenants were made prey to abstract rules created by remote courts that gave little deference to their views, needs, or consent, while the contract regimes enjoyed by the revolutionaries allowed them to rule their lives pursuant to *their* views, needs, and consents.

Similarly, as elites withdrew from the public schools, they positively insisted on ceding authority to *their* private school authorities to suspend children summarily for offenses deemed by consensus of their communities to merit swift discipline. How inappropriate it was, then, for such elites to have taken pride in rights regimes they had created at public schools that compelled authorities teaching poor children to cross gauntlets of hearings, depositions, trials, and appeals before even the most menacingly disruptive child could be disciplined.

A Reformed Legal System

Elites ought not to impose regimes on the poor that they are unwilling to live under themselves. Making such a quintessentially moral principle operative requires rejection of the patronizing notion that elite wardship over the lives of the poor is helpful to the poor. It calls for a legal system that permits local community institutions to be led by people with broad discretion to *restore* the "fetters of middle-class mores." It will require the legal system to recapture its once-strong bias in favor of contract regimes and its once-modest practice of being as attentive to the costs as to the benefits of its intrusions. It compels a system that adopts medicine's healthy rule: first do no harm.

Such a world will again permit ghetto principals and urban police officers and public housing officials and even welfare administrators to have sufficient discretion to draw lines defining appropriate conduct and to be held accountable by their communities when doing so—even as elites might have drawn different lines to govern the conduct of their communities. Such a world will be more concerned with now-common street drug bazaars that ravage ghetto communities, more alive to *overall* effects when it righteously protects "idlers. . . [from] the whim of any police officer." It will hardly regard it as "self-evident" that an overriding danger exists when poor people are barred from public buildings "because their appearance or hygiene is obnoxious to others." Such a world will hardly be perfect, and abuses will occur within it, but it offers hope if for no other reason than that it will empower poor people and their communities to escape the failed, patronizing, and virtue-indifferent regime of lawyers, under which they have lived during the past three decades.

Such a world may also offer public civic institutions a last chance to receive general public support and can provide the best hope for revitalizing urban centers no longer able even to fantasize that massive infusions of tax dollars will arrest their decline. It can provide a laboratory in which to test the visions of such rigorously honest supporters of large government as Mickey Kaus, whose book, *The End of Equality*, acknowledged that government can no longer redistribute income while remaining competitive in an economy now based on mobile entrepreneurs, mobile capital, and world markets. At the same time, Kaus saw government's central role as restoring a sense of community to an increasingly fragmented society—a goal he believed could best be achieved through the very public institutions that the rights revolution has weakened and made unattractive.

Experience with the rights revolution has painfully brought to light *Goldberg*'s fallacy: that greater process rights and more secure entitlements to welfare payments pose extraordinary dangers to poor communities. It also helps reveal a wiser, more deeply rooted constitutional principle: that real freedom and the promise of human dignity come from allowing people to shape the communities in which they live. The tools of constitutional lawyers can of course do much and will forever be essential to ensure the full citizenship and broad empowerment of all. At the same time, lawyers must recognize the down-to-earth reality of community freedom and self-determination.

There is a final, critical element in the history of the rights revolution—the ease with which its proponents laid claim to being the persons most committed to justice, most caring about minorities and the poor, most committed to offering them greater hope and opportunity, most attentive to our better angels. They acted as if they were the only ones who cared and were powerfully reinforced in this claim by the silence of those who disagreed with their agenda. Those who believe that poor people are best served by a humbler legal order, and those who understand the risks of utopian regimes, must never again allow themselves to be painted as indifferent to the poor. The tragic failings of the new rights regime were abetted by sins of omission among those who knew rights regimes for what they were but failed to assert a competing vision. Their torpor (and, to be fair, their smaller numbers) opened civic space for one-sided debates and made it too easy for the rights revolutionaries to capture the legal process.

Based on that history, those who believe that public and private conduct *should* be fettered by specific civic virtues can no longer indulge the luxury of failing to contest vigorously the prevailing vision, that of the rights regime, as the reactionary force it is. They are obliged to oppose its profoundly antipoor, antiblack, anti-community effects. They are obliged to define and strongly defend their vision of a proper legal order, more closely focused on the virtues necessary to local communities.

Such vigor, nothing less, will *recreate* the mediating structures that best protect against the abstract impersonality of rights regimes. It will best protect the autonomy and integrity of communities for whom the American dream needs most to be fulfilled.

7

Philanthropy and the Welfare State

Leslie Lenkowsky

I n November 1994, Americans elected a new Congress, whose leaders declared they wanted to see philanthropy play a larger role in solving the country's most pressing problems. They also floated the idea of making radical changes (such as allowing taxpayers to direct a portion of what they owe to charities) to help nonprofits do so. What, one might ask, was the reaction of leaders in the philanthropic world to this expression of confidence in them? Protest, dismay, and outrage bordering on hysteria.

We do not have the resources to do what will be asked of us, said nonprofit spokesmen, especially if the new Congress makes good on its pledge to cut welfare benefits and other federal programs. Some charities will do better than others in attracting funds, others added, leading to a "hodgepodge" of services rather than a "uniform approach." The "traditional partnership" between government and the nonprofit world will be at risk if the Contract with America goes into force, one writer claimed. And the real losers, wrote another commentator, will be "Americans who have been vic-

Portions of this chapter appeared in a slightly different form in the *Chronicle of Philanthropy,* January 12, 1995.

timized by birth, circumstance, or race." Since philanthropy cannot provide it, "where will the money come from to save those people from starvation, illness or death?" asked the Rev. Fred Kammer, president of Catholic Charities, USA.[1]

It is hard to envision any other sector of American society reacting quite this way to finding itself the object of political favor. (Imagine how America's farmers—or defense contractors—would have responded if the new congressional leadership were talking of giving them a pipeline into the federal treasury!) But for the philanthropic world, cries and protests when politicians talk of giving it more responsibility have now become *de rigueur*. In part, this is merely good business. Adversity is often the mother of donation, and the prospect of a Republican Congress's laying waste to social programs while demanding that nonprofits pick up the pieces is already becoming a feature of fund-raising appeals. Judging from what happened in the 1980s, when charitable giving rose by one-third in real terms amid howls about Reagan-era budget cuts, the results are apt to be good. Many Americans actually seem to like the idea of philanthropy's having to take on more responsibility (and government less).

Ironically, that is not what most leaders in the philanthropic world like. During the past thirty years, nonprofits have developed a mutually useful and rewarding relationship with the federal government for dealing with a wide array of national concerns. Government programs now provide over one-quarter of nonprofit revenues, while also giving their work a stamp of validation that helps elicit private contributions. At the same time, government has largely relieved charities of the burdens of performing certain kinds of activities they used to do, such as supporting single mothers or feeding the hungry. To reciprocate, many charities have become adept not only at carrying out government priorities but also at advocating more extensive public programs.

Seemingly for all concerned, this "partnership" has been a good deal. Hence, the cries of opposition when the new congressional leadership talks about changing its terms. To much of the philanthropic world, a cutback in government social welfare activity presents a threat, not an opportunity. But in truth, both for nonprofits and for those they seek to serve, the partnership has been a Faustian bargain that ought to be reexamined and renegotiated.

Philanthropy before the Great Society

Largely until the Great Society, philanthropy had a more distant relationship with the public sector. As Tocqueville famously observed, "association" usually preceded government in the new communities along the American frontier. Charitable groups came into being to do what public officeholders could not or would not undertake, such as educating the young or helping soldiers captured or wounded in war. This was not just a matter of necessity but also, in many cases, reflected the view that voluntary organizations were likely to be more effective than government bureaucracies, especially in providing relief for the needy and caring for the sick. In any case, widespread agreement that the public sector had a limited role to play in American society left considerable room for private philanthropic initiatives of all sorts.[2]

In his widely read essays on the "gospel of wealth," for example, Andrew Carnegie enumerated a variety of projects that he felt would provide the best uses for a millionaire's "surplus" holdings. These included creating universities, libraries, hospitals, medical schools, parks, concert halls, and public swimming pools.[3] Most of those would today be deemed enterprises requiring substantial government initiative and funding, with philanthropic resources perhaps playing a subsidiary role. But in Carnegie's time, they were worthy objects of private benevolence. Moreover, when Carnegie insisted that community support be available to maintain these establishments (as he did for his libraries), he mostly had in mind subscriptions, donations, and volunteers, not tax revenues.

As ideas about its acceptable scope changed, the public sector itself entered several of the areas Carnegie had identified. Yet even so, separate spheres of activity for government and philanthropy generally remained the norm. The most important New Deal social welfare programs, such as public housing, social security, and the Work Projects Administration, were run entirely by government agencies. Conversely, on matters where the public sector was lagging, such as the treatment of Southern blacks, private philanthropy stepped into the breach, including underwriting reports highly critical of official policies. As late as 1970, the Commission on Foundations and Private Philanthropy, a private body chaired by Peter G. Peterson, could still see this division of labor as one of the strengths of American society. "Autonomous islands of private philanthropy existing side by side with a system for public funding," its final report asserted, "provide indispensable initiatives for change."[4]

Third-Party Government

By this time, however, seismic forces in the form of Lyndon B. Johnson's Great Society legislation were already pushing the islands into one another. Unlike the New Deal, many of the social welfare programs of the 1960s used nonprofit agencies, not public bureaucracies, to achieve their objectives. Instead of creating government-run health clinics, Medicare and Medicaid were set up to reimburse private hospitals for taking care of the elderly and the poor. Likewise, many of the War on Poverty initiatives, such as Head Start and the Community Action Program, were run through grants to nonprofit organizations. New programs in the arts and higher education further obscured the boundaries between government and the philanthropic world.

This development of what Lester M. Salamon has called "third-party government"[5] was meant to serve a variety of purposes. By using nonprofit agencies, government policy makers hoped to administer their programs with more skill, creativity, flexibility, and perhaps deniability than a public bureaucracy allowed. In addition, for some of what they wanted to do, bypassing local political leadership was essential. Enlisting (or even creating) nonprofit organizations not only enabled them to take such a risky course but also gave them potential political support when elected officials complained.

The philanthropic world saw advantages in this new arrangement, too. First, of course, was the money, large amounts of it that, at least initially, appeared likely to expand the impact of what they raised privately. At the same time, a closer relationship with the public sector offered protection from the charges of elitism that were repeatedly leveled against segments of the philanthropic world, especially during the 1960s. When accused of being merely creations to serve the interests of the very wealthy, private foundations and charities could now cite their engagement in a wide range of "democratic" enterprises.

Perhaps most important, particularly to large grant makers and national nonprofits, an alliance with government seemed the most effective way to fulfill what they had gradually come to think of as their proper mission. Instead of merely responding to instances of need, these charities had embraced a broader project: to change society in ways that would eliminate the causes of need.[6] Their goal was no longer simply to be instruments through which communities could voluntarily come together to work on common problems but rather vehicles to change the communities themselves in order to end their problems. What better way to do so—indeed, given their limited capacity, was there any other?—than to join forces with a public sector similarly inclined.

By the mid-1970s, another study group, the Commission on Private Philanthropy and Public Needs, headed by John H. Filer, could report that "government has emerged in the United States as... *the* major philanthropist in a number of the principal, traditional areas of philanthropy."[7] This was largely a statement about the growth of public spending in areas in which nonprofits had traditionally held sway. It also implied the view, however, already widespread among leaders of the philanthropic world, that their fate was inextricably bound up with the continued growth of government.

The Price of Partnership

Thus, the alarm was raised over the prospect of cutbacks in the size and scope of the public sector. Despite being offered more responsibility (and even more generous tax treatment for donations), the nonprofit sector has so closely identified its interests with those of government that it regards these changes as potentially more harmful than beneficial. Yet, in so doing, it ignores the damage that has resulted from the past thirty years of partnership with the public sector.

In return for all the income and recognition they have received from government, nonprofits have paid a steep price: a loss of independence. In relatively small matters, such as accounting and personnel practices, they have become entangled in the red tape endemic to government grants (such as procedures for determining overhead or the appropriate length of hospital stays) and have been required to comply with rules (like those dealing with hiring or admissions practices) that are costly or even at odds with their own convictions. On larger issues, embracing government has often caused an organization to reconsider how it runs its programs—whether, for example, it can allocate more money to men's sports than to women's or create a religious atmosphere in a home for foster children—and opened it to repeated audits and other reporting requirements that strip away much of the privacy (and informality) that the private sector once enjoyed.

In more than a few cases, the partnership has also brought with it controversies and scandals that have harmed the organizations that were supposed to benefit. Stanford University, which was, to Andrew Carnegie, a model of what private philanthropy should create, has more recently become an object lesson in how a nonprofit's relationship with the public sector can besmirch its reputation.

Long before Newt Gingrich arrived on the Washington scene, many nonprofits had already become almost single-mindedly interested in the ebbs and flows of government budgeting. To prevent financial shortfalls, organizations have not infrequently tailored their activities to meet the priorities of government grant programs rather than their own sense of what might be worth doing. (Some have even employed lobbyists to assist in obtaining funds.) As a result, the supply of empty hospital beds, struggling symphony orchestras, and stupefying research projects is larger than it might otherwise be.

Few publications are as closely watched as the *Commerce Clearinghouse Daily*, which lists new government RFP's (requests for proposals). Special guides have even been produced to tell the understaffed nonprofit how it can find government grants. At many large charities, maintaining good government relations has become at least as important as developing good programs. Indeed, according to a recent Towers Perrin survey, the top government affairs official commands the fourth highest average salary in major nonprofit organizations, far ahead of the top program position.[8]

If all this had nonetheless helped the disadvantaged, restored blighted neighborhoods, or successfully addressed their other concerns, the new partnership into which nonprofits have so willingly entered might have been worthwhile. But that hardly seems to be the case. To the contrary, many in the nonprofit world are among the most vocal in pointing out that the number of Americans needing help seems to be greater than ever. Without the partnership, of course, matters might have been much worse. Yet with it, the opportunities for trying new approaches are much fewer than they would be if charities were less inclined to do it government's way. While judgments about the extent of variety and innovation in the philanthropic world are inevitably subjective, the heightened tendency of national nonprofits and grant makers to keep their eyes on

the public sector—even to synchronize their priorities with its—
has almost surely resulted in more similarity in how they deal with
poverty, medical care, education, and other issues of concern—and
perhaps less success as well.[9]

In expanding the partnership, the philanthropic world has done
more than merely seek grants. It has actively sought to shape the
programs that distribute them as well. Large foundations, such as
Ford and Robert Wood Johnson, have underwritten projects designed
to serve as models for national public policies.[10] Other nonprofits
have become accustomed to (and skilled at) participating in the legislative and administrative arenas in order to have their favorite
ideas written into law. (The most successful among them, such as,
ironically, the Points of Light Foundation, have even managed to
obtain line-item appropriations in the federal budget.) In doing so,
such organizations are behaving no differently (or more objection-
ably) from businesses or others seeking favors from government.
But they are continuing to blur such distinctions—and the value
attached to them—between the public sector and the nonprofit one
as remain.

Not that this is a matter of great consequence for many in the
philanthropic world. For what has ultimately fueled the growth of
the partnership has been an increasing similarity in outlook between those who affect policy in the public sector and their counter-
parts among nonprofits. Whether with regard to poverty, the arts,
education, health care, or other areas, the two groups have come
largely to share certain assumptions about the causes of the problems that concern them and the most desirable solutions to them.[11]
As a result, they are less concerned about maintaining separate
spheres of operation than they are about pooling resources and effort to promote their collective vision of what should be done. (To
assist in this, the Clinton administration, shortly after taking office, established liaisons for nonprofits in the White House and major
agencies.) And rather than foster a variety of independent approaches to dealing with public problems, they are more eager to
ensure that all are singing more or less the same tune.

In short, instead of creating synergy among organizations with
different strengths, the partnership has become a dysfunctional
marriage that leaves each party worse off. Although the nonprofit
world continues to benefit financially, its capacity to address issues
of concern to it is no greater and may even have diminished. Although the public sector has acquired an influential group of con-

stituents who support expanding its programs, its reputation for effectiveness and creativity—which its nonprofit partners were to help provide—is at a low. With such results, it is little wonder that calls for reexamining the partnership are now being heard.

Reexamining the Partnership

Such a reexamination might indeed result in nonprofits' being expected to do more, but it would also give them more freedom to try innovative ways of fulfilling such expectations. It might indeed eliminate or drastically alter a number of federal programs, but far from increasing the burdens on charities, such changes might diminish them by ending what many believe are counterproductive government policies. And far from hurting them financially, a new kind of partnership might even lead to an increase in their revenues that more than offsets the loss of government subsidies.

During the 1980s, Lester Salamon and Alan J. Abramson of the Urban Institute produced a series of widely noted studies that concluded that reductions in federal spending during the decade would greatly hurt nonprofits. They argued that the loss of both direct support for charitable organizations and government funding in "areas of concern to nonprofits" would create a burden that increased private giving (or other sources of revenues) would be hard-pressed to carry.[12] In the nonprofit world, their estimates were often cited as evidence of the need for emergency funds and the like to overcome the Reagan administration's effort to rethink the partnership.

In a much less noticed study completed in 1994, the same authors reviewed what had happened through the end of the Bush administration.[13] It turned out that growth in private giving during the period more than offset the loss of federal support for nonprofits. (According to their way of estimating, private donations grew by $69.6 billion during FY 1982–1992, while federal funding of nonprofits declined by $40 billion.) Furthermore, using a broader measure of federal spending in "areas of concern" to nonprofits,[14] the growth of charitable contributions still amounted to nearly 70 percent of the cumulative budget reductions. Despite the cries of doom (or perhaps even because of them), the nonprofit world managed to hold its own.

To be sure, some charities undoubtedly fared better than others during this period. But the result was a mixture of funds that reflected the public's concerns rather than those of bureaucrats, lobbyists, and agency heads. Revenues from fees also grew, suggesting that nonprofits had become more consumer-oriented as well.

A new partnership, relying less on government grants, may well leave some worthy causes short of money or place a premium on marketing abilities. That is already the case in the philanthropic world, however. (Indeed, the current partnership often leaves out important groups, such as religious charities, which would usually have to abandon the spiritual commitments that make them effective in order to participate.) A new partnership would undoubtedly produce a different ordering of priorities in the nonprofit world but not necessarily a poorer one.

Unfortunately, that is not what most leaders in the philanthropic world believe.[15] So closely do they identify their efforts and goals with those of government that the prospect of having to take more responsibility is unsettling. So accustomed have they grown to government grants that they cannot envision subsisting with fewer of them. So accepting have they become of the constraints imposed on their freedom of action that they are fearful of losing them. Sadly, the greatest obstacle to a reinvigoration of communal association and problem solving in the United States may well turn out to be the charities themselves.

8

The Corruption
of Religious Charities

Marvin Olasky

> *If I speak in the tongues of men and of angels, but have not funding, I am only a resounding gong or a clanging cymbal. . . . Now there are three ways in which government programs have harmed religious charities: by supplanting, by regulating, and by corrupting. But the most subtle of these is by corruption.*

Recently, I read to beloved Benjamin, my youngest son, one of the books he had picked out at the local library. Benjamin at age four judges books by their covers, and *The Duke Who Outlawed Jelly Beans* looks good: its cover features a boy in a crown speaking from atop a large bird as seven children of various nationalities and skin colors listen. The stories within, starting with "The Frog Prince," have good opening action and colorful pictures. Once each story is underway, though, insinuations begin to appear, and soon something unnatural this way comes: one child has two "fathers," another has two "mothers." Unlike the infamous *Heather Has Two Mommies*, a book that with its title is a setup to be taken down, *The Duke Who Outlawed Jelly Beans* proceeds subtly—as does some of the most pernicious influence of government on religious charities.

Supplanting, regulating, corrupting. . . . Clearly, over the past six decades, governmental antipoverty work has supplanted religious efforts. I have written about this trend at length elsewhere and have come to the conclusion that bad charity drives out good. Church-based homeless shelters that offer spiritual challenge as well as material help, for example, have a hard time competing against government-financed shelters, especially when the latter do not conclude that some lifestyles, such as alcoholism or drug addiction, are inferior to others.[1]

Clearly, regulation has also had an impact. Numerous rules can stare down a small church just as they can any small business or nonprofit. One recent book on the subject of church hiring and volunteer selection has a table of contents that would intimidate many local pastors: "Negligent Hiring Claims. Discrimination Claims. Equal Pay Act. Family and Medical Leave Act. Americans with Disabilities Act. Immigration Reform and Control Act." And that's only part of the federal legislation section; there are also chapters devoted to state laws and rules such as the "Handicapped Persons Protection Act. Discrimination against Any Person Possessing Sickle Cell or Hemoglobin C Trait. Department of Labor Regulation Barring Discrimination against Persons for Use of Lawful Products." In theory, religious groups may be exempt from some of the rules, but experts conclude that, despite the Religious Freedom Restoration Act, courts "applying secularist values and notions are likely to easily find compelling government interests that justify the intrusions into religious liberty."[2] Prohibition of sex discrimination or sexual preference discrimination is a likely suspect.

The government thus throws around its weight both by supplanting and by regulating. Yet, the saving mercy is that governmental offensives in both these areas can readily be watched, now that we are on the lookout for them. The third kind of harm—corrupting—may become in many ways the most serious because it is the least obvious. What happened between 1987 and 1992 to one religious charity in my town, Austin, Texas, provides a cautionary example.

The official story of the transition was one of onwards and upwards. Happy talk news reports in 1992 told of how, five years before, homeless Marion Morris had inspired a group of Austin church volunteers to start an organization called Helping Our Brothers Out (HOBO). Morris had dreamed of a place where homeless men could get their lives in order and where volunteers would offer one-to-one help. Reporters, to show that Morris's dream was still alive, displayed HOBO's 1993 budget of $689,000 (up from $28,000 in 1987, $146,000 in 1989, and $479,000 in 1991), with three-fourths of the money coming through government grants.[3]

It was hard to look askance at the success story, which was evident in the services HOBO could offer to transients who spent their days in HOBO's downtown building, rented from the city of Austin for $1 per year. Phones, mail service, haircuts, sack lunches, arts and crafts classes, and recreational activities were available. Movie showings were a particular highlight: on one afternoon when I visited, half a dozen homeless men were gathered around a television and VCR to watch *The Fisher King*, starring Robin Williams as a homeless man. A graduate student of mine who volunteered at HOBO—she put movies in the VCR every Friday and passed out popcorn and potato chips—wondered about the showing of *Basic Instinct*, in which Sharon Stone shows a lot: "It's a very provocative, sexy movie, and it was strange with lonely men watching it during the middle of the day. . . . They liked it."[4]

Liberal reporters who visited HOBO generally came away asking, "What's not to like?" In the words of Bob Schwab, a University of Texas economics graduate who in 1990 succeeded Morris as HOBO director, "Marion Morris never completed high school. We're the ones who have made good on his promise. When I first visited here I saw a clothing rack four feet long. Now we must have one 400 feet long."[5] And yet, some aspects of the official story I heard raised questions in my mind. Was HOBO's ascent along its original course? Why were former members of the HOBO board of directors a bit embarrassed about the direction of the organization they helped to create? And why had Marion Morris, the founder, disappeared from Austin? Further interviews with some of the principals eventually produced answers.

Alton Dyer's Tale

In 1986, Austin's Central Assembly of God church (located about seven miles northeast of downtown) had a program in which four dozen or so homeless people were picked up and taken to the church every Sunday morning. There they could take showers, attend a special service for homeless individuals, and eat a dinner on tablecloths. Marion Morris, former pastor of a Corpus Christi church, was one of the men attracted to that service. Although he was not homeless (he was living for free in a small house in exchange for renovations he was making), Morris certainly had gone through hard times since his divorce in the early 1970s. Approaching fifty, with a pattern of erratic work in the oil fields and the revival fields, Morris had little to show for his life. Then Morris and his long-term friend, Alton Dyer, had an idea. Hear Dyer's story:

> Marion was a preacher from the time he was 14 and a Pentecostal youth leader. He built him a big church in Corpus, was making good money, and had him a five-bedroom brick house on the bay. . . .

> He come home one afternoon and found his wife up and left him, went way up north somewhere. That's when his life started down. . . . He did odd jobs and then was doing good hauling saltwater from the oil fields, was married again with $79,000 in the bank, but he put the money in a nonprofit account saying it was for his ministry and didn't pay taxes on his income. . . . And he was out of church and was hitting the booze, and the IRS confiscated all he had, and his second wife went up north, and Marion started pastoring a little church in Luling. . . .

> I had been a drunk for thirty years, on the streets a lot of that time, and in the pen three times—theft over $50, hot checks, I tried to kill people when I was drunk. I wanted to go to a revival and change my life, and I was told there was one in Luling. . . . Happy Jack Gideon was running it with Marion, and Marion wasn't living right, but the true word of God hit home, my hair stood up on my arms, and I told God, "If you put me and my family back together, I'll never drink another drop." And since April 27, 1981, I haven't drunk a drop or been out of church. . . .

> Right after that Marion had some other work and so did I and we was friends. But Marion flopped up a job in Luling and had to move out of his place or he would have been on the street. . . . HOBO publicity says he was a street person but Marion never lived on the street—a woman here in Austin gave him a house to live in if he would fix it up. . . . I was here too, and we got to going to Central Assembly of God, which had its ministry for street people. . . .

> I knew how to talk with those people—when they hear someone say, "we want to help the poor," dollar signs get in their eyes, and they don't want real help, they just want more booze. And Marion knew how to get good Christian people stirred up. . . . I showed him the streets. We went to one building where hundreds lived in there with all

kinds of human waste. . . . Marion had clear thoughts. We had between us $47, that's all we had, but we got to pounding them streets and Marion said, "We can't do much with $47, but we can hit the churches. They'll pitch in."[6]

Morris was right. His pitch, as summarized by Dyer, was simple:

We was HOBO—Helping Our Brothers Out, 'cause in the Bible we're all brothers. The government wasn't going to be involved in it, the Christian people was gonna get the street people off the street, saved, and working. . . . Soon there was hundreds of volunteers that donated their time to HOBO, and churches taking up "love offerings." We had real people involvement, and we was changing lives. . . .

Then the politicians. . . got involved, and board members wanted more. And soon there was talk about getting government grants. . . . We didn't have no more business getting a government grant than the man in the moon. We didn't need it. We had this people involvement. . . . And there was big dinners at fancy hotels to raise money. The politicians was there, and money guys were on board, and Morris was telling me how broke he was. I said, "How can you be broke, going to all these fine hotels all the time?" He said, "That's what you gotta do to be big time."

And Marion couldn't handle the big time. His second wife left him and he got back on the bottle—I could smell the booze. He loved it when he went on television and people sent him money. . . . I'm not against money—it sure helps, and at HOBO now they got showers, there's a barber there, legal aid, everything you want. But now we can't have God in it nowhere. . . . Now that the government is involved, there's all that paperwork and all them rules. You can't do what you want to do, you have to do what they tell you to do. . . . Now, people bring clothes to HOBO and they send some money, but they're not really involved anymore. Now it's like the government.[7]

Bob Schwab's Story

What was tragedy in Dyer's eyes was enlightenment for Bob Schwab, who in both career and method was the antithesis of his predecessor. In college, Schwab decided to dedicate his life to the antipoverty movement. "That's the career for me," he said. "I could have built washing machines, but the poverty industry—the antipoverty profession—was something I wanted to do. It could give me a comfortable living—I wouldn't be rich, but I never wanted to be rich."[8]

Schwab said he began paying attention to HOBO soon after its birth in 1987. When HOBO board members sought a federal grant to provide housing for homeless persons in 1989, there were strings attached, Schwab noted: they would have to downplay HOBO's evangelical emphasis and hire a professional administrator. Schwab, applying for the HOBO administrator's job, recalled board members asking, "Do we want to give up our grass-roots, religious orientation to get these federal funds?" The decision, Schwab said, was, "Indeed, they did. Here's how it worked. I told them, 'Women and children need housing.' I told them, if they wanted to be selfless, they had to divorce their own beliefs from their program. . . . I told them, 'Feed the hungry, clothe the naked, before you begin to minister to them.' I told them, 'Just focus on the needs of these people.' And they bought it."

Schwab's message—that religious beliefs were getting in the way of programs, that "selflessness" meant not evangelizing, that fulfillment of material needs comes before ministry, that "needs" themselves are defined as material—assaulted the heart of evangelical understanding. But once the board "bought" his message, Schwab had the job and the mandate to make changes: "My first day on the job, people would answer the phone, 'HOBO Ministries.' When I heard that, I was horrified. . . . This agency had received a federal grant, and would quickly be getting a city and county grant— and we were calling ourselves a ministry! I got all the people together and said that had to stop."

There were some complaints, but board members attracted to the government apple proffered to HOBO had already bitten in and changed bylaws to make the purpose of the organization "charitable" rather than "religious." Gary Thornton, an Austin lawyer who was chairman of the HOBO board when it hired Bob Schwab, said, "As HOBO grew, we faced a choice: either the organization would be a minor, church-related institution, or we could get grants that would force us to relinquish the religious ties. . . . Accepting grants meant that we couldn't help people spiritually, but. . . we saw the availability of funds. We saw people who could be helped. We had families involved with us that we'd have to put back on the street, unless we took the money."[9]

Accountant John Porterfield, an evangelical who was a board member during the transition, recalled in 1992 that

> we never decided to go out aggressively after grants, but we became aware of grants that we could just pick up. We knew there were strings attached, but... the money was there in our hands, the only question was whether we should put it in our pockets. It wasn't so much a specific decision to change the thrust but it was a recognition that physical needs have to be met, and that in order to do that we needed a much bigger infusion of dollars.[10]

Porterfield, according to board member Marion Coleman, a theologically liberal foundation executive, "wasn't happy about changing the bylaws. The bottom line for him, though, was, 'I want us to carry the Lord's message, but if it's the difference between having it upfront and having the money, we've got to have the money. We can still communicate it, but we can't define ourselves by it.'" Carrying the Lord's message did not prove to be so easy once it had to be done by stealth, however. Coleman recalled that "once we started getting the grants, we had to honor what we said we'd do: the religious climate at HOBO had to change. . . . We signed an agreement in the grant applications. We must honor separation of church and state. We cannot preach religion to these people.'" Furthermore, once the bylaws were changed, as Coleman noted, "we weren't a Christian organization any more, so it was inappropriate for us even to ask [potential employees] questions about religion."[11]

Porterfield, seeing the spiritual emphasis disappearing rapidly, tried a new proposal: "I wanted to set up a parallel entity alongside HOBO, so that we could take federal money with it but still keep ministry elements in the other. But I was probably late in suggesting that." Marion Coleman, speaking of her fellow board members, noted that "these folks felt like it was prostituting ourselves to take that money. But when you're in that situation, if you must make that kind of sacrifice. . . then that's the right thing to do."

Marion Morris's Story

After checking many false leads, I finally tracked down Morris in Corpus Christi, Texas, where he was back at the church he left almost twenty-five years ago. Here is his story:

Alton and I started HOBO with the idea that what worked for us would work for other people. . . . Alton had been on the streets for years, and I was facing the streets. For sixteen years before that I was struggling, ever since my marriage ended. . . . I had been in the limelight. I spent very little time with my family. . . . I bought off my wife with new cars, a five-bedroom house on the bay, lots of things. That just played out. . . . Came home one day, there was a note on the table. She wanted a divorce.

Then I started drifting. . . . Pastored a little church in Luling for two years. . . felt like I was faking it every day. . . . Then I got into the oil fields, made some money, bought eight row houses. . . . I was putting CDs in the bank in the name of the church in Luling, but I had resigned from that church. . . . The IRS was going to put me in the pen, but they discovered I was an ignorant preacher, not a crook. . . . I left Luling with 46 cents in my pocket. . . . I was a bitter, unforgiving man. I doubted my faith, doubted the existence of God. I tried to stay drunk, to hide the pain. . . . [I]t seemed like anything I touched turned sour. . . . [E]veryone was responsible for my problems but me. . . .

I set up HOBO based on my own experiences. The Bible teaches us that we sin because of the lusts of our own hearts—money, women, pride, whatever. We like to point fingers at other people—wife, the system made me do it. . . . Some people choose rightly, others make the wrong decisions and become homeless. . . . We need to repent and take responsibility. . . . Central Assembly of God had the right idea, but once-a-week wasn't doing much for the street bums, and it wasn't doing anything for Alton and me. So we figured out something else: we asked if we could borrow the vans. . . . We got fifty donated uniforms. . . . We grabbed guys on the street who wanted to work. We got really busy hustling jobs for people and then we took the guys to work—we worked unloading trucks, stocking shelves. . . mechanical work on cars, maintenance, cleanup work. . . .

The idea was that Alton and me would get a percentage of the pay. We never did get paid, but we got a pickup truck donated to us, and the sight of 30 homeless

men in pullovers, working, stirred up some interest. We
planned a dinner for the homeless on the lawn of the
Capitol. We asked for a permit to serve 200. . . . 1200
came. HOBO took off. . . . What we understood is that
people on the streets don't just need clothes and food.
When they hit the streets they lose their families, so we
tried to link them up with their families. . . . We tried to
get them to think about God, and about their own sins
and their own responsibility. . . .

We wanted individuals to get involved in helping,
not just by sending checks but on the basis of using their
own talents. If you're a barber, cut some hair. If you're a
dentist, fix teeth. If you're a doctor, heal some sores. . . .
We linked people with people. The doctor not only gave
the gift but saw the result of the gift. Nothing can compare with that.[12]

The board, the bureaucrats, and Bob Schwab destroyed HOBO
in its original understanding, Morris said, and he blamed himself,
in part, for not thinking ahead:

I went after some of those people for the board because I thought HOBO needed credibility. But when those
professional people got to rubbing elbows with homeless
people they got very uncomfortable. . . . [T]hey understand
paper and organization, but they don't understand street
bums. . . . The board was growing weary with me because
we did a lot of things that the rules and regulations didn't
provide for. . . . We picked up old food for people to eat,
better than they were getting from dumpsters, but the board
feared lawsuits from people being poisoned. . . . And some
board members didn't like it that we were an evangelical
organization, that our whole purpose was religious. . . .

When [new manager Schwab] done away with all
the church people he done away with the program. But I
couldn't fight much. My second wife left me for one of the
guys on the street. She rented an apartment and put him
in that apartment. Then I was really bitter. . . . I tried to
ease out of HOBO. . . . Now, it's completely changed. . . .
You get in line and fill out an application. We wanted
volunteers, but now there's a paid staff, good salaries,

and the government money goes into the pockets of a few bureaucratic people. . . . It's more money down the drain. The government's been doing for 50 years what HOBO does now—throwing money around, building welfare programs. That's no good.[13]

HOBO Transformed

Early HOBO should not be glamorized. When it began operations in an old downtown building in 1987, about 100 homeless people on cold nights would pack it with not only their bodies but also their addictions. Barney O'Connor, a retired carpenter who was HOBO's night watchman, recalled that "there were jealousies and fights. I carried around a big sheath knife. Never had to use it. Showed it a lot."[14] And yet, after a year, rough edges still showed, but procedures were in place, and churches were supplying both material and spiritual challenge. HOBO's message at that point could have been summarized as:

> Find a job. Learn that you are created after God's image and should have a goal other than a nasty, brutish, and short existence. Do not be yourself, if your self has become entirely selfish, and shortsightedly so at that.

That message was very different from the post-1990 HOBO message of making it easier for homeless individuals to maintain their chosen lifestyle, whatever it is. (The subtext of the message that no lifestyle is necessarily superior to any other is that there is no reason for homeless men to change their behavior.) The HOBO transition was unusual except in its rapidity: what took place in three years there took decades to accomplish in the United States generally. But HOBO had the advantage of a late start, which often allows newcomers to leapfrog long periods of preparation and become thoroughly integrated into governmental structures in an amazingly short time. Just before the 1992 presidential election, HOBO sent out a "press release and photo opportunity alert" announcing the inauguration of a program by which HOBO staff members were deputized to register the Austin homeless to vote. The political had replaced the personal.[15]

HOBO brochures early on had defined HOBO as "a ministry. . . . We're the formerly homeless helping the current homeless." But on election day 1992, a HOBO brochure publicized its funders (including the U.S. Department of Housing and Urban Development, the Texas Commission on Alcohol and Drug Abuse, the City of Austin, Travis County, and the Austin Community Foundation) and the agencies housed in HOBO's resource center (including Legal Aid, the City Health Clinic, the Texas Employment Commission, the Foundation for the Homeless, the Department of Veteran Affairs, and the alphabet soup-like ACC Education Services Providing ABD/GED). The combined resources of these organizations made it seem as if HOBO had gained the whole world—and the cost of the conquest was forgotten.

The problem of HOBO's change, for those who care about effectively helping homeless men, is more than theoretical. Effective compassion throughout American history has been challenging, personal, and spiritual; HOBO after a year had all three components in place, but by its fifth anniversary had lost them. Was the loss inevitable? Had Morris not been battered by personal problems, had the board of directors been better chosen, had HOBO's board of directors not succumbed so readily to the lure of big governmental bucks, or had some creative organizational alternatives been developed early in the process, perhaps the slippery slope would have had some sand scattered on it; perhaps HOBO would not have fallen so far, so fast, as it rose financially. But the story of twentieth-century antipoverty work is that bad charity supplants the good, bad charity imposes regulations on the good, and bad charity corrupts the good. HOBO's hobbling is high-speed history.

Repeatedly, the lure of governmental funds has made it hard for organizations to remain dedicated to compassion that is challenging, personal, and spiritual. Board members who have become involved in poverty fighting because their hearts were touched are forced into a terrifying choice: supply material help to many, using government funds, or supply spiritual help to a few and suffer nightmares about those who slipped away. Were men angels, they would choose rightly, with faith in God's providence—and some have done exactly that—but we should not be too hard on those who care enough to fail the scary test. Rather, one goal of those who care about mediating structures should be to change Washington's rules so that religious charities are freed from discrimination not only overt but subtle as well.

9

Success Stories

Robert L. Woodson, Sr.

S cholars, policy analysts, and public officials have now acknowledged the value of a mediating-structures paradigm, which
stresses the important role of social institutions such as families and neighborhood associations in sustaining the cohesion of
communities and buffering individuals from the anonymity of the
larger society. Both the Left and the Right have embraced the notion that intermediary institutions in society can play a crucial role
in guiding the behavior and influencing the value-based choices
people make as they go about their daily lives. The word *empowerment* has become a common term in the lexicon of public debate; yet
policy reform has not kept pace with verbal support.

From 1977 through 1982, during my tenure as a resident fellow at the American Enterprise Institute, I sought to demonstrate
how mediating structures have played a key role as resident community "antibodies" in maintaining the health and stability of
America's low-income neighborhoods. Two books were produced from
this research, *A Summons to Life* and *Youth Crime and Urban
Policy: A View from the Inner City*. In gathering information for
these publications, I contacted many of the community leaders with
whom I had once worked, this time not as a fellow activist but as an
objective researcher. I conducted hundreds of interviews with former
gang leaders, ex-drug addicts, and others whose lives had been trans-

formed as a result of their relationships with community leaders in their neighborhoods. I wanted to document what it was that gave grass-roots leaders the ability to engender a change in the values and choices of these people that enabled them to accomplish a turnaround that would salvage their lives. I was searching for the operating variables that effective community leaders of all races and ethnicities shared. How was it that they could be effective with their meager resources while well-funded, professionally designed and managed interventions of the welfare state had failed?

Grass-Roots Activism versus Custodianship

Time and again, I found that indigenous community leaders have substantial long-term impact because they have been able to affect not only the behavior of those they serve but also the internal base of values that determines behavior. In tackling the most critical problems that confront low-income communities, they have made distinctions—as most top-down programs do not—between poverty that is caused by factors outside an individual's control (for example, layoffs or extended illness) and that which results from the life choices an individual makes (drug addiction and out-of-wedlock births, for instance). They recognize that, with regard to poverty that results from an individual's choice, an internal change is prerequisite for any external programs or aid to have lasting and substantial effect.

Grass-roots activists who live within the same zip code as the people they serve have a unique capacity to inspire this kind of transformation. In many cases they have suffered—and have overcome—the same problems that they are guiding others to battle. They are often living examples of achievement against the odds, and they provide models of the values and principles that they espouse. Hundreds of testimonies from effective grass-roots leaders have shown that their foundation of faith has enabled them to see potential for transformation and revitalization where professionals have limited their goals to custodianship.

Furthermore, surveys have shown that a base of local support is a more natural and more approachable resource than professional services that are "parachuted in" to the communities. When queried, hundreds of low-income people responded that if they confronted a crisis they would turn first to family members, friends, local churches, and other organizations that are indigenous to their communities for help. Only as a last resort would they choose to turn to a professional service provider.

In spite of this reality, we continue to use a service delivery system that relies on what is the last choice of those who are in need. Evidence abounds of the failure of an approach that relies merely on behavior modification or therapeutic intervention. A recidivism rate as high as 60 percent has been reported for boot camps for delinquent youths. Not long ago one newspaper reported the story of a juvenile offender who simply walked away from a $100,000 per year therapeutic center in a resort town to return to the inner city and commit a second murder just blocks from his first. As trillions of dollars continue to be infused into the bureaucracy of an ill-conceived, massive service delivery system, conditions of the poor have continued to deteriorate.

Effectiveness of the Local Community

In sharp contrast, the effectiveness of local community leaders was verified in my second book, *Youth Crime and Urban Policy*, which focused on grass-roots efforts to end gang violence. This book was based on three days of panel discussions with fifteen former leaders of street gangs and their adult sponsors. These forums were attended by sociologists Peter and Brigitta Berger and Robert B. Hill. The testimonies in these meetings described remarkable transformations as groups of young people who had once terrorized their communities became agents of peace and stability in their neighborhoods. Grass-roots activists (many of whom had, themselves, once been involved in gang violence) were able to work through a central point of influence, the gang leader, and to redirect the energy and creativity of hundreds of youths.

The youths' personal accounts were hailed by the *Vanderbilt Law Review* as "a powerful testament to the plight of the dweller of America's crime-plagued inner-city neighborhoods" that "gives the reader the power of voices from the street—voices of people who are daily trying to stem the tide of despair, decay and crime that surrounds them."

After leaving AEI, convinced of the primacy of mediating neighborhood institutions, I founded the National Center for Neighborhood Enterprise (NCNE) as an action-oriented organization that would advance the work of community leaders and their organizations. NCNE not only documented the successes of neighborhood-based initiatives but also helped to sustain and expand grass-roots efforts through training, education, and technical assistance. In the course of thirteen years, NCNE's network has expanded to include hundreds of community leaders, serving thousands of low-income constituents in thirty-eight states.

NCNE has also provided forums in which grass-roots leaders have come together to share the strategies they have found to be effective and to identify any administrative, procedural, or regulatory barriers that have impeded their progress. Their firsthand experience provides valuable guidelines for policy reform that could strengthen the mediating structures of low-income neighborhoods and remove regulatory obstacles that have hindered their efforts. The following profiles will provide a sample of the effective strategies that have been implemented by grass-roots leaders to address problems ranging from drug and alcohol addiction, to youth crime, to the steadily rising number of births to unwed teens.

My enthusiasm about the victories that have been claimed in our nation's most afflicted neighborhoods is tempered only by a frustration with a prevailing elitism that has failed to lend substantial support to the efforts of these dedicated community leaders. It is not surprising that liberals have ignored the victories that have been won on the grass-roots level. Those who are now in control of what has become a virtual poverty industry will not readily cede their domain to competitors whose goal is solving rather than "maintaining" the problems of the poor. But it is especially disappointing that substantial support for community leaders is not being offered from conservatives who have given lip service to the concepts of self-determination, personal responsibility, and the value of mediating structures.

On the basis of their track records of proven success, and because their constituents trust them and seek them as a source of support and guidance, indigenous community leaders should be considered the primary vehicle for the delivery of services and resources to their neighborhoods. Moreover, the invaluable firsthand experience of grass-roots activists who have worked "in the trenches" and won victories over some of the most critical problems that now face our nation should provide guiding principles for any policy discussion that concerns the issues that affect their communities. Their input should be a fundamental part of the formulation of policy to address the needs of America's inner cities and impoverished rural areas. It is my hope that this publication will be an important first step in making this a reality.

Generating Community Revitalization

Toni McIlwain of Detroit, formerly a homeless mother of three, worked days and studied nights to achieve self-sufficiency and, ultimately, homeownership. Having struggled and sacrificed to move into a community where her children would have a chance for a better future, she was incensed to witness drug dealers' gradually moving in and taking over her neighborhood.

Toni refused to accept the options of submitting to the take-over of her community or moving to another neighborhood. As powerful as the drug dealers may have been, she reasoned that there was strength in numbers and that one crack house should be no match for the other thirty-five households on her block. Determined to salvage her neighborhood, she knocked on each door with hopes of rallying at least a critical mass in an organized effort to shut down the crack house.

In the beginning, most of the neighbors were reluctant to get involved, and some were suspicious or irritated by her efforts. Her first organizational meeting was held in a nearly empty room. But Toni persisted, and by the time of her fifth meeting, there were evident interest and cooperation from the community. When the drug dealers realized that her efforts were taking root, they threatened her, and on one occasion a gunman disrupted one of the neighborhood gatherings in her home. But momentum was growing, and the residents' new-found resolve could not be shaken.

A project to promote safety in the community was launched. Thirty-five of the thirty-eight square blocks in the neighborhood were organized with block captains and supporting officers, and a neighborhood security patrol was created to work in conjunction with the city's police department. Today, crime in the area has dropped by 40 percent.

The residents of the Ravendale neighborhood take pride in their cooperative revitalization efforts and have named themselves the "Ravenites." Pooling their resources, they have been able to purchase a number of former crack houses for the costs of their back taxes. They then invested their time and talent in a cooperative effort to refurbish the properties, applying their skills in carpentry, plumbing, and painting.

Toni also took initiative to rally support for the neighborhood's efforts from other sources. She made arrangements with a hardware store for donations of paint, which was used to improve the former crack houses as well as the homes of residents, which were painted by teams of neighbors. In addition, she helped to create an adopt-a-block partnership project that linked residents of her inner-city neighborhood with the congregations of suburban churches. The partnership not only provided support through a fellowship of faith and friendship but also grew to include a number of cooperative community development activities. As a fitting testimony to the success of community activism in Ravendale, a nature park stands today on the site of one crack house that has been demolished. In what was once an area of intimidation and danger, landscaping and benches now offer a place for relaxation and recreation in a thriving, peaceful neighborhood.

Fixing the Homeless

For ten years, in the heart of Denver's skid-row district of Larimer Street, a small building has been the site of a program for the homeless, "Step 13." Since it was founded, Step 13 has served more than 2,000 men and women, 35 percent of whom are now holding jobs and renting or buying their own homes.

A key to the program's remarkable success is the vision and experience of its founder, Bob Cote. Cote, a former alcoholic who once lived on the streets himself, recognizes that an essential starting point in developing a solution to homelessness is to identify the source of each individual's problem. He stresses the importance of disaggregating the population we have labeled "the homeless" and addressing the causal factors of each person's situation.

For some, homelessness is due to situations beyond their control—job loss or sickness. Others wander the streets as a result of mental illnesses. But for the majority of the homeless, the root of the problem lies in addiction—to drugs or alcohol. It is to this population that Cote has committed his efforts.

From firsthand experience, Cote well knows the needs of his clients and has designed a program that is fundamentally different from conventional shelters, which he refers to as "warehouses for the homeless." He explains, "Any system that takes responsibility away from a capable person dehumanizes that person."

Step 13 requires each of its residents to work to contribute to the maintenance of the facility, usually $120 a month. Residents may begin with $4.00-an-hour jobs at Step 13. On the basis of a track record of responsible effort, they graduate to jobs with local businesses with whom Cote has made arrangements for pay ranging up to $13 an hour.

Step 13's residents submit to random urine testing for drugs and alcohol, and some receive Antabuse, a substance that produces nausea if alcohol is drunk. In Cote's words, "You don't just give a street drunk a bed and a meal and some money. He knows how to work the system too well. You've got to get him out of his addiction."

The failure and waste of a government program that subsidizes addictions as "disabilities" provide vivid proof that Cote is right. Under the auspices of the Social Security Administration, more than 80,000 drug addicts and alcoholics are currently receiving Supplemental Security Income checks (SSI), which average $446 a month. A report recently released by the inspector general of the Department of Health and Human Services revealed that the average recipient has been on the rolls for 7.4 years, that only 1 percent of the alcoholics and addicts who receive these benefits ever recover or get jobs, and that the vast majority are dropped from the rolls only when they die or go to jail.

For Cote, SSI stands for "some sort of insanity." He has witnessed many cases in which the checks have been sent to a third party—liquor stores where the recipients have standing accounts. He reports that the day the checks arrive is known on the streets as "Christmas Day." Noting that the recipients he knows hold onto their checks for no more than four days, Cote says the program is equivalent to supporting "suicide on an installment plan." Frustrated with the waste and damage caused by the system, Cote remarks, "People are afraid that the homeless will freeze to death in the winter, but they forget the hundreds who die on the streets in the heat of the summer from dehydration and overdoses." In sharp contrast to the SSI "beneficiaries," many of Cote's graduates are now earning above $20,000 a year and own homes and cars.

As Step 13 residents progress to more substantial jobs, their living quarters also change. Step 13 participants begin living in barracks with a number of roommates and then progress to semiprivate rooms and, ultimately, to private rooms that they can furnish as they please. This progression stimulates a dynamic of role models or, in Cote's terms, "constructive envy." He explains, "Many of these guys know each other. They've crossed paths in the jail, on park benches, at the detox facility, or in the hospital. When they see one of their peers who has been working buy a nice car or move into a room with a phone and a 23-inch television, they respond." One former resident whose construction talents were discovered through his work with Step 13 now owns his own home, car, and a thriving construction company that provides jobs for new entrants in the program.

Because Step 13 takes no government funds, it is free from regulations that limit a client's length of stay. Some of Step 13's residents need to stay with the program from one to two years to make sustainable progress. Cote stresses, "You've got to give these people a chance to get sober and stay sober. You can't take someone who's been sleeping under a bridge, drunk, every day for five years and expect him to get turned around in 30 days or by keeping him in a shelter for a few nights and then putting him back on the street with a donut and coffee."

As difficult as it may be at times to secure a steady flow of funds to meet his operation's needs, Cote knows what works and would not trade his freedom to design the program as he sees fit in return for government funds. In his words, "[With government funding] I'd have to have three psychiatrists and ten therapists to tell me why these people are homeless. I know why. The problem is alcohol."

For hundreds of men and women, Cote's focus on the root cause of their problem and his demand for personal responsibility have been key to an escape from years of dehumanizing dependency.

A Safe Haven and Springboard for Success

For many children growing up in inner-city public housing projects, survival itself is a victory. In the Parkside housing development in Washington, D.C., one woman, Rita Jackson, could not sit passively and witness the future of a generation of young people crumble in an environment where teens trade sex for drugs in darkened hallways and police open fire with drug dealers across playground lots.

Rita grew up in that community, and she knew that there were ways to grow and gain nourishment. As a young girl, she had bravely boarded a bus each week that took her across town to a neighborhood of strangers where she would attend dance and drama classes. For her, this opportunity had built her self-confidence and broadened the view of her world, and she wanted to offer the same experiences to the youths in her community.

In 1979, beginning with just eight students—with total commitment, indefatigable energy, meager resources, and a prayer— Rita launched the Northeast Performing Arts Program. As the children publicly performed dance and drama routines, more and more young people pleaded to join the program, and her ranks steadily increased.

But Rita's involvement with the youths went far beyond that of a dance instructor. She functioned as a rare confidante with whom many of the children could share their experiences. She heard the tragic accounts of little children who first witnessed drug abuse in their own kitchens by their mothers, of others who were helpless in the face of sexual abuse perpetrated by relatives or "friends" of the family, and of young boys and girls who lived in constant fear of drug posses that had permeated their neighborhoods. Rita's sincere response won their trust, and in time her humble public housing unit gained a reputation as a safe haven in the violent environment.

As in the parable of the loaves and fishes, Rita stretched the groceries she had to provide supper for those who gathered in her living room to listen to music, watch television, and share their problems and their dreams. Often, especially during summer months, a number of the youths spent the night, sleeping where they could find room in the safety of Rita's home.

With a selfless desire to meet the children's needs, Rita continually generated new projects to promote the spiritual, emotional, and physical health of the young people who came to her. She organized field trips to the monuments, museums, and public cultural events that many public housing children never see.

Having sparked the self-confidence and vision of those she served, Rita went on to develop the College All-Aboard Program to encourage the young people to pursue higher education. This project provided information, resources, financial aid referrals, grant and scholarship information, and assistance in filling out college applications. To date, through her efforts, more than eighty youths from this one public housing community have gone on to college. Rita also realized that, scholarships or not, living expenses would always be needed by her students, so she launched the Young Entrepreneurs Succeeding Program, which taught the basics of market research and financial planning. A number of small businesses were then launched by Rita's students. One, a balloon company, netted one young entrepreneur $3,000 during her summer vacation.

As college-bound youths moved on toward their futures, Rita tapped the talents of these young protégés in raising up the younger children through a project called Save Our Seed. This mentoring program provides young people with positive role models, lessons in constructive conflict resolution, and career counseling.

Since 1979, the Northeast Performing Arts program has touched and changed the lives of more than 800 young people. Most have stayed in touch with Rita and with one another, forming a network of mutual support that now spans more than five states.

Lodestar Victories

The victories claimed by dedicated community activists throughout the nation continue to multiply. In one year, the National Center documented the testimonies of more than 100 grass-roots leaders and hundreds of those whose lives they have changed.

Among these remarkable accounts was the story of Freddie and Ninfa Garcia, former drug addicts whose first "date" was a robbery of a convenience store for which Ninfa drove the getaway car. A series of personal tragedies and one ultimate moment of reckoning brought this couple to a point of conversion and dramatic change.

Freed of their addictions, they committed themselves to reaching out to others who were captive to drug and alcohol abuse. Together, they founded a rehabilitation program, Victory Outreach, which has grown to include a residential facility, drop-in center, family support sessions and individual counseling, a prison ministry, and a hospital ministry. Since its inception twenty years ago, Victory Outreach and its sixty-five satellite ministries throughout the Southwest and South America have successfully rehabilitated more than 13,000 drug addicts and alcoholics.

The accounts of a nationwide network of grass-roots activists should provide more than moments of inspiration for those who read them. These stories of victories should become a lodestar for the design of a new approach to solving the economic and social problems that face our nation. These neighborhood leaders should be at the table when the design of any solutions to the problems that confront their communities is discussed.

An important first step to acknowledging a new brand of "expert" in community revitalization would be research that would compare the costs and outcomes of conventional professional programs with those of grass-roots initiatives. It is my hope that such a project will be taken on in the near future, and it is my belief that such documentation would be a milestone in a continuing and growing endeavor "to empower people."

10

Practical Principles

Stuart M. Butler

Other chapters in this volume identify threats to the role of mediating structures, some willful but most resulting from well-meaning attempts of government to assist such organizations. "The helping hand strikes again" is how Robert Woodson characterizes the disturbing process by which outside assistance can so distort the mission of a once-effective organization that it collapses or loses its purpose.

That distortion can be complete. The "little platoons" become so dependent on government assistance, and so cut off from their communities and original purpose, that they campaign against efforts to foster genuine mediating structures. Consider today's debate over the reform of welfare and other domestic programs. Proposals to shift more responsibility for delivering social services from government to mediating structures are bitterly attacked as unfair and naive by the large charities, most of which receive a significant share of their support from government and are thus anxious about budget cutbacks.

If we are to foster true mediating structures so that they can play a greater role in American life, how can we do so without undermining the purpose and characteristics of the very organizations we seek to encourage?

The first step to solving this puzzle is to ponder who are the "we" who should be determining which mediating structures should be used or strengthened. The term *empowerment* gives a clue to answering this question. The most important "we" are those people whose lives are intimately bound up with those institutions. These are the people from whom in most instances the mediating structures evolve, and they are the people the institutions are meant to serve. Be it church, community group, or even family, the ultimate indicator of usefulness and worth of a mediating structure is whether ordinary people rely on it or seek to rely on it. So perhaps the most important task is to figure out how decisions on which organizations should be used and strengthened can be put more firmly into the hands of the people who will be most affected by their activities.

But there is another "we," namely, the wider community or society, which also has an active and legitimate interest in the matter. The generally regarded leadership of a community and those with the greatest resources have traditionally been called on to take part in the selection and support of efforts to strengthen mediating structures. To be sure, the vision and resources needed to create or assist an important mediating structure have often come from reaching individuals and institutions within the community—even governmental institutions—that do not rely significantly on its services. In this case, a wider, or "public," purpose is the motivating force. The history of American communities is rich with examples of civic-minded individuals who form associations to promote a common interest in helping particular groups of people. But as other authors in this volume have emphasized, there is a danger in this. Financial assistance from political bodies, and even large private donations, can often push institutions away from the path that qualified them as true mediating structures.

Most troubling of all are the concerns associated with government as the instrument of "we," the wider society. Government is distant: it does not have the intimate knowledge of a community organization that local people have, so it can be misled and choose unwisely. Government is also subject to pressure from constituencies that feel threatened by a greater role of mediating structures, so its decisions to help or harm may be politically motivated. These features of government have made it a poor instrument to help the institutions that are meant to be a bridge between the individual and the wider society.

Some have argued, in the context of welfare reform, that the deficiencies associated with government support can be dealt with by devolving government decisions to the states, through block grants. The idea is to move decision making to levels of government that are closer to the people. But while there are many good reasons to move social programs to the states, it is by no means clear that this reform alone would foster the growth of mediating structures—it may even impede it. States, in fact, are just as subject as the federal government to pressure from special interests who feel threatened by mediating structures—and more so in some places. This susceptibility to pressure at the state level is why so many of the regulations and legal barriers frustrating mediating structures emanate from state governments. State welfare bureaucracies also tend to be even more hostile to innovative community-based institutions than federal officials.

How, then, can one select an appropriate mediating structure and draw upon its unique qualities to address shortcomings and opportunities in society, *without* undermining the qualities that make the institution so valuable? The observations of other authors in this volume suggest a possible set of practical principles.

Don't Decide—Let the People Decide for You

Discovering which organizations are truly effective and responsive mediating structures is difficult, especially for a public or private donor from outside the community. Those who purport to be representative of deserving mediating structures, or who would give advice on behalf of ordinary people, often turn out to lack any real base of support. As Edmund Burke reminded us, "It is a general error to suppose the loudest complainers for the public to be the most anxious for its welfare." Forgetting this maxim has permitted many worthless organizations to grow fat with government help and favorable regulation while many effective organizations struggle to exist in a sea of red tape or shrivel up for lack of necessary support.

One way to reduce this danger is to channel outside financial assistance through the beneficiaries of organizations rather than directly to those organizations. So the "we" deciding which institutions will be supported become the individuals who will rely on those mediating structures as links to the broader institutions of public life. To gain financial assistance under such an arrangement, the organization must be able to win the support of those individuals.

As one way to achieve this result, vouchers have been proposed or introduced in such areas as education, housing, day care services, and health care. Vouchers require organizations to "market" themselves directly to those who will be served rather than to those who ultimately provide the financial support (typically government). Despite the attractions of vouchers and similar ideas, there are legitimate concerns that need to be addressed if the general approach is to work well.

One is that placing ultimate decision making into the hands of beneficiaries works better for some services than for others. In education, there is wide agreement that parents, on behalf of their children, can and should exercise the power of choice. But the issue is not so simple when the individual's ability to make informed decisions is in question. Should drug addicts undergoing treatment have complete freedom to choose which organizations shall serve them? That may be better than the alternatives in many instances, but there would be plenty of opportunities for exploitation.

Another concern is that accepting a voucher may turn out to be a poisoned chalice for an organization, encumbering it with heavy regulation. This is of particular concern to private schools in the debate over education choice. Nonetheless, vouchers appear to carry much less of this danger than direct forms of government support.

Look for a Community of Interest between the Server and the Served

Robert Woodson talks of applying the "zip code" test to those who claim to serve or advocate for the poor. By this he means that anyone giving support to an institution should first find out if those making the claims reside in the same neighborhood as those they say they are helping—hence the zip code test. While hardly definitive, it focuses attention on the important point that a mediating structure should be truly *part* of the local community, given that its purpose is to be a link between individuals and the larger institutions of public life. Mediating structures are not, as some seem mistakenly to believe, any nongovernmental institution offering to serve a community.

The importance of this distinction is explained bluntly by Kimi Gray, who led the movement to achieve resident management of public housing projects. Why, she was asked some years ago, does a group of tenants manage a project better than a professional management company? Because we manage ourselves, she said, and so have a strong personal reason to do the best job possible. "The engineer lives in the project. When the heat goes off, he gets cold too!"

The general principle here is that a true mediating structure must have an intimate involvement with the community it serves. Its leadership is either directly of that community or at least shares a common experience, if not literally a common zip code. This helps explain the general success of organizations such as Alcoholics Anonymous or antigang programs headed by former gang members.

Public and private bodies wishing to encourage mediating structures need to remember this crucial local aspect. An organization may be public spirited and dedicated, but if it is not truly part of the community or does not truly have a common bond in some other way (such as a religious belief or shared experience), it rarely qualifies as a genuine mediating structure.

Look for Results and Local Support, Not Credentials

As others have shown in this volume, the most innovative and effective mediating structures are usually the creation of people who on paper are unqualified. Thus if government agencies and private philanthropic organizations are to help finance these cutting-edge institutions, they have to find ways to discover and verify organizations that are very short on resumes and whose application forms contain many blank spaces.

This poses a dilemma for funders, particularly public funders. How do funding officials discharge their fiduciary responsibility, ensuring that money goes to qualified, bona fide organizations and yet also direct funds to the most deserving new institutions? In the real world, even an insightful funding officer has to justify his or her decisions to a supervisor, auditor, or oversight committee chairman who will see only the paperwork associated with a funding decision. The pressure on that officer is to show traditional credentials and long experience in a group he has funded. The fiduciary responsibility thus invariably runs counter to the urge to assist the more creative but least "professional" mediating structures. And this dilemma is made more difficult by the tactics of the professional organizations who see "amateur" groups as competitors for funding. Not surprisingly, these professional groups lead the demand for credential requirements to "protect the public" from "unqualified" organizations or individuals.

While not an easy dilemma to resolve, there are two possible approaches. One is to use the services of intermediaries to identify and verify effective mediating structures, drawing on the special knowledge these intermediaries have of the communities involved. These intermediaries might even be called, inelegantly, "mediating structures for the mediating structures." But even this approach has its dangers. Federal agencies and philanthropic foundations wishing to help the poor have a distinct habit of taking advice from intermediary organizations with little interest in fostering the use and growth of mediating structures. Still, it is much easier and more efficient for an agency or private funder to verify thoroughly the integrity of a small number of such intermediaries than to be successful in a widespread effort to find or determine the value of small, local organizations.

The other approach is to recognize the parallels between the creation and evolution of innovative mediating structures and the same process in the business world. Innovative, small start-up firms also tend to look questionable on paper. And significantly, they do not tend to receive their early capital from banks or the U.S. Small Business Administration—the equivalent in the commercial world of philanthropic foundations and government human service agencies. Outside money instead comes from friends and relatives, people who know firsthand the potential of the business owner.

This parallel suggests additional principles that in part recognize the limitations and dangers implicit in the financial support of mediating structures by large public and private institutions. It also suggests that we should explore ways of reducing the everyday costs of organizations and reinforce the importance of encouraging help from those who *know* the organization.

Reduce Costly Barriers Rather than Forcing Organizations to Raise Money to Overcome Them

As other authors have shown, most innovative and effective mediating structures face a host of costly regulatory barriers, usually erected by officials who have little comprehension of how such organizations actually need to function or are even hostile to their activities. Many regulations, such as those often applied to day care, education, job training, or housing management, seek to block mediating structures from even offering services in competition with existing public or private suppliers.

Removing these restrictions would substantially reduce the operational costs of mediating structures, helping them very directly by cutting the money they need to function. Reducing such regulations and licensing requirements, moreover, would also make it much easier for ordinary people to turn to mediating structures in preference to other institutions. And a bonfire of restrictions would make it much easier for organizations with a track record and community support in one area of activity to repeat their success in another area.

The deregulation of mediating structures may well be much more important to these institutions than finding new ways to fund them. Regulation is the tool used by opponents of mediating structures to block their growth, and the political device used to prevent money flowing to innovative organizations that challenge the status quo. Thus regulation is at the heart of all today's political debates over the role of mediating structures, whether it involves education, housing, welfare, or other social services. In the debate over reform of the social welfare system, opponents of change will seek to preserve rules and press for new ones to shut out mediating structures or raise their cost of operation. Those who believe in empowerment will have to battle regulation every step of the way.

It Is Better for Government to Encourage Individuals to Support Organizations Directly than for Government to Fund Organizations Itself

As other authors in this volume have made clear, accepting money from the government all too often has a profound and damaging effect on mediating structures. Invariably, it encourages, or even requires, organizations to surrender their special character and position in society as they seek to comply with government requirements. By making these organizations less concerned with satisfying the local community, and more sensitive to the demands of a distant official, it weakens their relationship with that community. Government money also carries with it many operational mandates that reduce the real value of each dollar received. And, of course, government uses its own criteria in selecting mediating structures to receive help, which are not the criteria of those most affected by the organizations.

But this does not mean that government can play no role in strengthening the finances of mediating structures, other than by reducing costly regulations. For one thing, it can leave more money in the pockets of ordinary Americans, letting them allocate that money to the organizations of their choice rather than taking that money and then forcing people to use organizations of the government's choice. This philosophy is at the heart of proposals to reduce taxes on families in tandem with reductions in government funding for social services—including cutbacks in grants to non-profit groups to provide those services. The central issue in this approach is not about whether it is a good idea to spend money on school lunches or other services or whether nonprofit organizations should be funded. The central issue is *who* should control that spending and decide which institutions should receive support. Allowing Americans to keep more of their earnings permits them to exercise that control and decision making. Organizations could then receive support with little or no regulation but with the crucial requirement that they justify themselves to the people who part with their own money.

To spur support further, government could build on the current tax relief available for charitable donations. Making changes in the tax laws at various levels of government could make such contributions more attractive for moderate and lower-income Americans through a tax credit system or by easing the rules governing tax-free contributions. In addition, there are proposals to allow taxpayers to "vote" to allocate some of the taxes they pay to specific social service organizations. Thus, rather than trying to help by taking money from the people and then allocating that money according to the criteria of officials, government could in these ways help by giving ordinary Americans greater freedom to support the organizations of their own choice.

In the first edition of *To Empower People,* Berger and Neuhaus pointed out the central importance of mediating structures in today's America, as Tocqueville did in the America of his time. Most Americans agree that these institutions are vital to society and want policies to encourage them. But these policies must be designed within a framework of practical principles. Those, in turn, must recognize the important fact that mediating structures are an outgrowth of the individuals who compose discrete communities and should be dependent always on these individuals for their continued existence. Whenever well-meaning efforts to use or strengthen mediating structures ignore this principle and "free" them from the final judgment of ordinary people, such efforts sadly serve to weaken these invaluable institutions.

11

Bottom-up Funding

Douglas J. Besharov

When government uses a particular mediating structure to advance its social welfare purposes, it funds specific activities through a grant (or contract) made directly to that organization. Known as "third party government," this form of assistance has become a substantial proportion of total government spending for noncash social welfare programs. And the social service arms of many mediating structures have grown accordingly.

Unfortunately, government often selects the wrong mediating structure for the job. And even when it chooses the right one, its assistance often comes with entangling strings that threaten to destroy the very characteristics that make that mediating structure effective. That is why many thoughtful observers decry all government assistance to mediating structures.

Some services (residential care and health care, for example), are too expensive to be funded by the private sector alone, however. If mediating structures are to perform these functions (and many would say that they should not), ways must be found to help them escape what other chapters in this book call "government's fatal embrace." This chapter argues that the dangers caused by government funding of mediating structures can be lessened by an approach to funding that is "bottom up" rather than "top down." In fact, a bottom-up approach has much broader benefits, and it would be easier to institute than many people imagine.

Do the protections afforded by a bottom-up approach outweigh the inherent hazards of government support to mediating structures? As we will see, the answer probably depends on the specific situation (especially since government often regulates mediating structures, even when it does not provide financial support). But readers will have to judge for themselves.

Three Axioms

The first principle set forth in Stuart Butler's chapter presents the starting point for this chapter's discussion. He writes, "Don't decide—let the people decide for you." Before I describe how this principle might be implemented, it may be helpful to emphasize certain axioms implied by his advice.

1. Direct government funding of social welfare agencies (including mediating structures) is likely to create the wrong winners and losers. The process is analogous to establishing an industrial policy: that is, government tries to pick the best service provider (instead of the best manufacturer, for example). Unfortunately, governmental decisions are less likely to be correct than are the cumulative decisions of thousands, or millions, of consumers. Worse, once government funding begins, political pressures make it almost impossible to end support. Thus, in his research on the differences between private and government support for start-up companies, Allan Meltzer found that private decision makers were more successful because they were more likely to abandon an obviously unsuccessful project than was the government. In other words, government is not capable of performing the key aspect of good decision making: creating losers.[1] Many Head Start providers, for example, were chosen for reasons having little to do with their ability to care for children—and many others continue to be funded even though they are pale reflections of their former selves.

2. Direct government funding of social welfare agencies can alter the nature of their services and raise their costs. When government chooses the service (or agency) for clients, it often imposes costly quality standards on the service. Since government tends to impose regulatory standards with less regard for whether they result in a better service than do individuals (who must pay for the service out of their own pockets), government-supported services or programs tend to be more expensive than those that individuals purchase themselves. And government often decides that it knows how to provide the service better than the actual provider, so that it often requires even successful providers to alter their programs. No better example of this two-sided dynamic exists than the quality-cost differentials between publicly and privately funded child care.

3. *Direct government funding often requires mediating structures to abandon the very features, like religious activities, that make them effective.* Of course, the government, through its police power, always has the authority to regulate the activities of mediating structures even when not giving them money (subject to various but limited constitutional constraints such as the right to the free exercise of religion).[2] But the temptation to attach requirements to the behavior of mediating structures—and the political support for doing so—is greatly increased when there is direct funding. After all, goes the argument, the money is public money and must be spent in accordance with the "public trust."

What I have described as direct government funding can also be seen as top-down funding.[3] That is, the money is transferred from the government[4] to an agency that, in turn, provides services to its clients. But what if individual clients could make these funding decisions? Although some might select inferior services, they will do better than government on average because they are in a better position to determine what they need and because their individual decisions are less likely to be determined by extraneous factors (such as political favoritism). Thus, the cumulative impact of their decisions would likely establish a stronger cadre of services.

Moreover, if individuals rather than government bureaucrats were selecting programs, there would be less chance that institution-distorting strings would be attached. The defunding of apparently unsuccessful services or programs would also be easier because consumers would simply stop selecting them.

Thus, one way to protect mediating structures is to create mechanisms that transform cumulative consumer demand *directly* into funding for their activities (that is, without an intervening governmental decision). This chapter examines four methods of achieving this sort of bottom-up funding: (1) cash assistance; (2) lower tax rates; (3) vouchers; and (4) reimbursement for copaid services. It then describes the various situations in which one or the other mechanism seems most appropriate and the residual dangers that they all pose to mediating structures.

Cash Assistance

Cash assistance can be used for those purchases that can be made in the open market with minimum supervision of the consumer. Cash assistance maximizes consumer choice and requires no special regulation of providers. In addition, giving cash allows individuals to spend less than might have been anticipated on the service and to use the difference for other purposes. (This approach creates downward pressure on their individual expenditures, on total expenditures, and also on the price of goods and services purchased.)

Cash assistance can take the form of a cash grant to specified clients, an automatic tax benefit for designated classes of taxpayers, or an across-the-board tax cut.[5] The best-known cash approaches are probably Aid to Families with Dependent Children (AFDC) and the tax exemptions for dependents. The House Republican proposal for an increase in the exemption for dependent children under eighteen is an example of using the tax code to provide cash assistance for general purposes.

Food stamps, which are discussed next, are usually considered to be vouchers. Food stamps, however, are increasingly like cash because there is now a black market for purchasing them. If recipients are willing to accept about a 20 percent discount off their face value, most are able to trade their stamps for cash, thereby escaping the need to spend the benefit only on food stuffs. Moreover, even when used properly as vouchers, food stamps have many attributes of a cash grant. Because clients are able to use them to purchase any number of different items, there are both relatively wide consumer choice and corresponding competition among providers.

Recently, welfare agencies have made cash grants available to clients in job training and work programs to pay for child care. Cash grants, as opposed to vouchers to clients or contracts to agencies, allow clients to purchase child care from a variety of informal sources, including family members. Although some advocacy groups feared that parents might seek out inadequate or dangerous placements (to save money), so far there is no evidence of this.

Lower Tax Rates

Many people would view *tax cuts*, for low- and middle-income families, at least as a form of cash assistance. Over the past thirty years, a greater portion of the federal payroll and income taxes has been shifted to low- and middle-income workers and to families with children. One of the main reasons for this shift has been the decline in the relative value of the personal exemption. Eugene Steuerle has provided some of the best analysis of this issue.[6] That greater tax burden on lower-income workers and families puts added financial stress on them and creates more pressure in two-parent households for both parents to work.[7]

Some experts justify this shift in tax burden on the basis that low- and middle-income families now receive additional benefits from the federal government. But why do we need to take money from families in order to give it back to them?

Taking money from families (or all taxpayers, for that matter) and giving it back to them in the form of categorical assistance is a way of controlling their spending decisions. So, for example, when tax funds are used to provide student loans to middle-class families, we are taking money from one pocket and putting it into another because we do not think that parents can (or will) save the money themselves.

This kind of forced saving, or intertemporal redistribution of wealth, sometimes makes good policy sense. Some degree of social engineering is probably inevitable. But we do it far more than we should, and with harmful results.

As we have seen, the process can easily get out of hand and can hook Americans on a never-ending upward spiral of tax increases to pay for programs designed to relieve the very burdens created by those taxes.

In 1993, for example, the original Clinton proposal to expand the Earned Income Tax Credit (EITC) proposed providing this "low-income" tax benefit to families earning almost $30,000—even as we tax the same families to help pay for the benefit. The administration quickly withdrew this proposal, although I must add that the current EITC has many problems that should be addressed.[8]

Vouchers

Vouchers force clients to use a specific service or provider (unless, like food stamps, the vouchers can be traded for cash or other services). The best examples are probably vouchers for housing and child care, since they are hard to trade or sell.[9] And since clients cannot pocket the difference between a lower-cost provider and the assumed value of the voucher, they have no incentive to be cost conscious.

Vouchers also increase the tendency of the government to impose standards. Generally, to prevent fraud in voucher programs, the government must designate those who may accept the voucher. (Again, food stamps are an exception, because of the large and competitive consumer market for food.) Since the service providers have to be approved, the temptation grows to regulate them to make sure that the money behind the voucher is not misused.

Contrary to popular impression, tax credits (and, to a lesser extent, tax deductions) are for most purposes more like vouchers than cash; that is because tax credits can be used only for a designated purpose (if one assumes that the purchases would otherwise not have been made). But what if the purchase would have been made anyway, so that the credit or deduction has no effect on behavior? Then, tax credits are more accurately considered a cash subsidy to a group of taxpayers who happen to behave in a certain way (or have certain expenditures). Thus, President Clinton's 1995 proposed tax deduction for college or other postsecondary education was at most a voucher and, as some complained, might have been no more than a subsidy to the upper-middle class (whose children would likely go to college whether or not its cost is deductible).

An interesting hybrid between cash and voucher systems is "grant diversion." Under this procedure, an individual's cash grant (under, say, Supplemental Security Income, SSI, or AFDC) is paid directly to a service provider (such as a residential drug treatment program), an employer (to supplement earnings), or a landlord (when rent goes repeatedly unpaid). Since the diversion is for designated purposes, the payment, although formally denominated in dollars, is more like a voucher. As efforts to reshape the behaviors of public aid recipients grow, we may expect greater use of grant diversions. A system could be established, for example, that allowed homeless individuals to use their food stamps and any other welfarelike payments to cover their housing and food costs. Christopher Jencks, in his book *The Homeless*, makes a similar suggestion.[10]

Reimbursed Copayment Systems

Reimbursement for copaid services rendered requires consumers to pay part of the cost of a particular service, often under a sliding fee scale arrangement. The government then "reimburses" the provider for the rest. Copayments are usually seen as a method of constraining costs or rationing services by making individuals feel the costs of their decisions (or at least to feel them partially). Thus, copayment schemes are most attractive when there is a need to encourage recipients to set priorities among what would otherwise be discretionary purchases. Today, they are most often seen in child care programs.

An unappreciated benefit of both total reimbursement systems and copayment systems is that they allow individual choice.[11] Thus, if structured properly, they can provide all the benefits of other bottom-up approaches. A rule could be established, for example, that over a designated period of time a minimum number of clients must select that particular service provider; otherwise, the provider is dropped from the list.

Ordinarily, a reimbursement system, such as Medicaid or Medicare, is subject to runaway costs because recipients have no incentive to economize and providers do not compete on the basis of cost. Copayment requirements help, but program costs are still hard to control. Hence, many programs adopt additional ways to restrain costs, such as by limiting the number of approved service providers (if the number of approved providers is small enough to restrict access). Medicaid uses this approach to limit the number of heart transplants it funds. Income-eligibility guidelines can also restrain costs by limiting the number of potential clients.

Conclusion

Except for lower tax rates, each approach described above can be applied to funding any mediating structure, from the family to organized religions.[12] And taken together, they provide a menu of approaches that reduce the risk that government assistance will prove to be a fatal embrace for particular mediating structures.

Nevertheless, except for cash, each approach does increase the risk of greater government control. Even when government does not provide financial support, however, this is a real danger. Government regularly uses its police power to regulate the activities even of the mediating structures it does not fund. (In most places, church-based day care is regulated even when no public funds are involved.)

There is, though, the other lurking problem with government funding of mediating structures. It builds a politically connected constituency for continued (and increased) government spending. In some areas, like education and health care for the poor, such spending is all but inevitable in the modern world; in others, constituency politics can drive up expenditures.

The trick, then, is to aim at balance. And the trade-offs vary by context. Medicaid and Medicare funding of church-related hospitals, for example, has created client-driven systems without changing the essential character of those institutions; the issue of mandating abortion services does arise regularly but is typically negotiated successfully.

There may be other funding devices we have not thought of yet. A surge of fresh imagination would certainly be useful.

12

Seven Tangled Questions

Michael Novak

Often it seems as if everybody in the discussion of "mediating structures" knows exactly what it is he or she wants. When several such persons sit down together to discuss their concrete plans, however, they often find that they do not have in mind the same things at all. "We'll never achieve this unless. . . ," one of them will begin. Another will interrupt him: "But what exactly is the 'this' that needs to be done? What is it that we're working for?"

Suppose someone says that we should promote more "choice" in education, more private schools, and somebody else says, "Yes, Catholic parochial schools have done spectacular work with far less money than the public schools; they should get more state support." But someone else butts in: "The main reason they've done better is that they don't now *receive* state support; state support is the last thing they need—it would wreck them."

There are many tangles of this sort. Just as an argument starts to go forward, someone brings up a counterexample that halts the rest of the discussants in their tracks. The objection is one they have not quite thought through. The categories they have been using do not quite handle it. The kind of question being raised demands a quite different framework.

To sort through some of these tangled nodes of argument, I have found it helpful to sort out seven different *kinds* of questions that arise in the matter of mediating structures. It is helpful for inquirers to recognize early on that they must learn how to think simultaneously on several different levels, tilted in quite different directions.

What Is the "This" We Are Seeking?

The question is, What sort of society are we aiming for? What is the "health" we are seeking, the "ideal" we are trying to realize, the "end" we are trying to reach?

I propose that what our hearts desire is a society in which the self-governing actions of individuals and their small local organizations grow in number and frequency. In this way, freedom will be *exercised*, not simply lie dormant. Citizens will become more and more active *subjects*, who imagine new things, who launch initiatives of their own, and who make course corrections by learning from the consequences of their own actions. We would also like to see the number of spheres in which such actions occur steadily increase.

Another way of putting this is that we would like to see a society in which the number of healthy, vital, and satisfied "little platoons" is steadily on the increase at society's base. We would like to see the spheres in which large bureaucracies make key decisions diminished. While we see the utility of large institutions' framing certain general rules in a way that all, or practically all, deem healthy for the common good, we do not like it when such bureaucracies intrude too often and too extensively into the concrete decision-making space best occupied by local agents.

There is a difference between framing general rules that, once clear to all, genuinely liberate individuals and their associations and a list of concrete, detailed dictates formulated by a bureaucracy. Such bureaucracies (especially but not only those of the state) treat people like clients, even like clients who lack common sense, good will, and a decent respect for their own duties, so that they need to be *told* what to do.

While we desire a larger proportion of daily life to be under the sway of local decisions, locally arrived at, and a smaller proportion to be made on more distant bureaucratic levels, we do not deny that there is a need for such organizations. Their help is something necessary or merely useful. In the late twentieth century, however, these higher bureaucracies have grown too powerful, too intrusive, and too arrogant even while claiming to be "good for us." That is why it seems necessary now to devolve more power back to the "little platoons." The higher authorities have become remote centers of impersonal power.

Our founders' ideas about the way of life necessary for a self-governing people—expressed in Thomas Jefferson's First Inaugural, for example—began to be abandoned with accelerating speed in the late twentieth century. In part, this trend was attributable to the hold of the socialist or statist myth upon many of this country's (and the world's) artists and intellectuals. While it is attractive to elites, this tendency toward bigger government has led to many unintended consequences, counterproductive results, and a corrosive cynicism about their own governing elites on the part of huge numbers of people. Listen to Jefferson again—his words like cool, clear water after a trek through a hostile desert:

> Let us, then, with courage and confidence pursue our own Federal and Republican principles, our attachment to union and representative government. Kindly separated by nature and wide ocean from the exterminating havoc of one quarter of the globe; too high-minded to endure the degradations of the others; possessing a chosen country, with room enough for our descendants to the thousandth and thousandth generation; entertaining a due sense of our equal right to the use of our own faculties, to the acquisitions of our own industry, to honor and confidence from our fellow-citizens, resulting not from birth, but from our actions and their sense of them; enlightened by a benign religion, professed, indeed, and practiced in various forms, yet all of them inculcating honesty, truth, temperance, gratitude, and the love of man; acknowledging and adoring an overruling Providence, which by all its dispensations proves that it delights in the happiness of man here and his greatest happiness hereafter—with all these blessings, what more is necessary to make us a happy and a prosperous people? Still one thing more, fellow-citizens— a wise and frugal Government, which shall restrain men from injuring one another, shall leave them otherwise free to regulate their own pursuits of industry and improvement, and shall not take from the mouth of labor the bread it has earned. This is the sum of good government, and this is necessary to close the circle of our felicities.

While a *democracy* naturally favors the self-governing little platoons of life, in a federal republic there is also a powerful countertendency to concentrate power in the central state. Similarly, it is the natural tendency of *capitalism* to inspire fresh waves of small entrepreneurs and many little platoons of new small corporations. But there is also a natural countertendency toward larger combinations, the formation of temporary monopolies (as when a new invention allows a firm a few years' advantage over other firms), and the growth of small firms into ever-larger ones. Again, it is a natural tendency of *pluralism* to generate fresh and original voices pointing out new directions, perhaps even several different contrary directions at once; but there is also a tendency in pluralism to degenerate toward the lowest common denominator. Indeed, in all three cases, there seems to be a certain ebb and tide first in the one direction, then in the other; first toward the large, then toward the small.

Still, it seems clear that the smaller institutions are those in America most in desuetude these days, having been overshadowed for some fifty years by the concentration of ever-greater powers in the hands of the national administrative state. A considerable devolution is called for. Better, perhaps: many experiments in devolution.

What Is the Funding Source behind Such New Arrangements?

Should the federal government continue to raise funds in taxes, which are then passed back to the mediating institutions and little platoons of life, so that they might accomplish their purposes? The danger is "Who pays the piper chooses the tune." We see many examples of *federal* "generosity" distributing its funds to local organizations in a way that actually corrupts them and alters their nature beyond recognition.

Should the *states* then become the funders of mediating institutions? But state governments, too, as well as the federal government, can corrupt, overcontrol, and distort the purposes of local institutions.

Shall the little platoons then throw themselves upon the generous instincts of the public, not entirely unlike mendicant friars of old?

It seems, for example, that a flat tax of, say, 17 percent, no exemptions allowed, would leave more income than at present in the hands of those who earn it. Recall the words of Jefferson quoted earlier: "Shall not take from the mouth of labor the bread it has earned." Citizens might well apply that extra income to social purposes that they themselves prefer, rather than to the purposes currently chosen by big government. It is likely that some things now being funded would not be funded—and the reverse. But would not lessons from local funding be more speedily learned? Would not the concrete effects of projects funded be more immediately felt? Such lessons, presumably, would speedily affect future giving patterns. Would that not be healthy?

Whichever funding scheme is decided on, there are a great many social needs, which self-governing citizens need to discern for themselves, decide to do something about, and effectively meet.

Is there already a large range of funding mechanisms that could be brought to bear on a broad and varied array of social problems? Do new sources and methods need to be invented?

What Is the Size of the Provider?

How large would we want mediating institutions to grow? Is there a useful role for such large organizations of the private sector as the United Way, Catholic Charities, the Red Cross, and others? Such organizations seem every bit as large and bureaucratic as large business corporations or entire branches of government. How ought we to think about them? How could the tasks they now perform be better performed by volunteers gathered in smaller units and facing more immediate and local needs? Are the only good mediating institutions small ones?

What Is the Role of Government?

In the United States, the term *government* applies not only to the federal government, and not only to the state governments, but also to other governments on a descending scale of extension: counties, cities, boroughs, townships, wards, neighborhoods, villages, and so forth. It is not altogether bad to be faced with such a dazzling array of possibilities. Which levels of government are more effective in solving which problems?

Current arguments in favor of defederalizing various kinds of welfare benefits, for example, and sending many welfare programs back to the states may leave out of account the fact that the states, too, often function as gigantic bureaucracies, possibly as blind and insensitive to mediating structures as the federal government has proved itself to be.

What Are the Organizational Methods and Modus Operandi?

There seem to be a great many ways in which to organize nongovernmental institutions, along with a considerable variety of available methods, even for organizations working in cognate fields. To many people today, it may seem more "progressive" to employ methods that allow the members of organizations to *participate* in decision making, even at the cost of many inefficiencies. Others (like me) abhor attending large participatory meetings, even (especially!) *small* committee meetings, and prefer to delegate decision making to individuals made responsible for particular functions.

Are there any telling reasons for being committed to one style of organization rather than to another? Should one specify a preference or allow as wide a variety of organizational styles as proves useful to those doing the organizing?

What Is the Ethos or Underlying Philosophy?

In some ways, the impersonal rules governing a bureaucratic organization can represent a "higher" morality than that found in organizations dependent on kinship, family ties, local loyalties, and informal custom. In certain remote clinics in a country of Southeast Asia, for example, nurses instructed to give out medicines to patients on certain fixed schedules responded more strongly to the moral obligations to their own families and resisted what they took to be merely "bureaucratic" rules. In some cases, accordingly, nurses kept medicines intended for patients and sold them in the marketplace, for the benefit of their own needy families. A family ethic conflicted with an ethic based on abstract rules and regulations.

There is no perfect form of organization. No ethos or organizational philosophy is without its inherent limits and counterproductive tendencies. In his essay in this volume, for example, Marvin Olasky tells the poignant story of how a very successful local organization for the homeless, led by two charismatic leaders, was taken over by a new team of leaders. The new leaders were certainly more "professional," smoother fund raisers, and more nearly in tune with other urban elites. The earlier leaders were more amateurish but had more dramatic results in the quality of lives changed. The newer team built a larger, shinier shelter tending to a greater number of clients.

One troop of Boy Scouts differs from another in morale. One set of local leaders is brilliant and creative; another set is quite ordinary in knowledge, imagination, and effect.

What Is the Role of Civil Society?

In societies under the grip of the Communist Party during the years 1917–1989 (and it is still so in such societies as remain), total control over social life was vested in the Communist Party. The principle of association was severely curtailed. Virtually the whole of social life was thoroughly controlled, and always spied upon, by the state, through the instrumentation of the party.

In resistance, those who opposed the Communist Party in Central Europe rediscovered the principle of "civil society." They learned through their own harsh experiences that a healthy social life cannot exist solely and only through the state; put otherwise, the realm of a healthy social life extends far beyond the boundaries of the state. It is necessary for the state to be limited, under the rule of law.

The term for all these nonstatist forms of social life—those rooted in human social nature, under the sway of reason—is *civil society*. That term includes natural associations such as the family, as well as the churches, and private associations of many sorts; fraternal, ethnic, and patriotic societies; voluntary organizations such as the Boy Scouts, the Red Cross, and Save the Whales; and committees for the arts, the sciences, sports, and education. Human associations come in a multitude of forms. Civil society is normally "thick" with many types of civic association. In free and complex societies such as those of Western Europe and the United States, a single individual is likely to belong to many different associations at once. Some are natural (the family), some are voluntary but enduring across generations, and still others are founded for limited purposes and are quite transitory.

In a sense, therefore, the "mediating structures project" is simultaneously a project in the strengthening of civil society, as defined over against the state.

Meanwhile, as the nations of Europe now struggle to build

new forms of federalism in creating a larger "European Community," a term that first entered common use in Catholic countries—the principle of subsidiarity—has come into common use to express the difference in roles between the communitywide authorities and the member sovereignties. In fear of the totalistic, all-absorbing state that the socialists were promising (there was, as yet, no existing socialist state), Leo XIII (1878–1903) began to talk about the relative autonomy of lower levels of government vis-à-vis higher authorities: for example, regional governments against the national government. It then fell to Pius XI in *Quadragesimo Anno* (1931) to formulate this latter principle clearly as "the principle of subsidiarity" as follows:

> The State authorities should leave to other bodies the care and expediting of business and activities of lesser moment, which otherwise become for it a source of great distraction. It then will perform with greater freedom, vigor and effectiveness, the tasks belonging properly to it, and which it alone can accomplish, directing, supervising, encouraging, restraining, as circumstances suggest or necessity demands. Let those in power, therefore, be convinced that the more faithfully this principle of "subsidiarity" is followed and a hierarchical order prevails among the various organizations the more excellent will be the authority and efficiency of society, and the happier and more prosperous the condition of the commonwealth.

In *Centesimus Annus* (1991), John Paul II formulates the principle with a different emphasis:

> A community of a higher order *should not interfere* in the internal life of a community of a lower order, depriving the latter of its functions, *but rather should support* it in case of need and help to coordinate its activity with the activities of the rest of society, always with a view to the common good [emphasis added].

It is worth noting that the Cambridge historian Lord Acton thought that the division of sovereignties between state governments and the federal government in the United States was one of the great steps forward in the history of liberty. Indeed, the post–Vatican II Catholic encyclopedia *Sacramentum Mundi* offers the following quotation from Abraham Lincoln as the earliest formulation of the principle of subsidiarity:

> The legitimate object of government is to do for a community of people whatever they need to have done but cannot do at all, or cannot so well do for themselves in their separate and individual capacities. In all that people can individually do as well for themselves, government ought not to interfere.

Lincoln's formulation, it will be noted, has an emphasis similar to Pope John Paul II's.

Related to civil society and the principle of subsidiarity is a third theme: the principle of association. In his opposition to socialism, for example, Pope Leo XIII frequently and insistently favored the creation of *private associations* that would undertake necessary social tasks, so much so that he became known as "the Pope of associations." After some hesitation, for example, he became the champion of labor unions; and he encouraged associations that would support the family, associations to work for reform on behalf of farmers, associations of artists and scientists, and the like.

Leo XIII laid emphasis, then, on what Alexis de Tocqueville in *Democracy in America* had earlier called "the law of association." Tocqueville called this the first law of democracy: when a free people sees the need for something to serve the civic good, free citizens organize themselves in associations to accomplish these tasks on their own. They do not turn to the state as people do in France, he said, nor to the aristocracy, as people do in England; in America, they turn to one another. In short, the law of association is a fundamental principle of self-government. A people that wishes to be self-governing, cherishing a limited state so that they might live as much as possible independently of the state, needs to develop the art of association to a very high level, in order to act effectively on its own behalf. The art of association, therefore, is a *condition* of proper self-government. It is, in fact, the daily work of the experiment in self-government.

Conclusion

As has already been suggested under the seven headings above, each solution to a human social problem seems to bring with it a schedule of failures as well as of successes. The fantasy of a future utopia must be ruled out. At whatever level of analysis one chooses, there is no perfect society. Therefore, whatever the pattern of mediating structures, little platoons, or instantiations of the principle of subsidiarity that one finally chooses to support, one probably ought to build in checks and balances internal or external to the system, as well as procedures for bringing about future adjustments and reforms. Sooner or later, each form of organization will reach its natural limits and begin to display inevitable weaknesses.

Those who see the promise of mediating institutions, then, have never promised a rose garden. In fact, some of them, being of a Burkean temperament, may well anticipate that fifty years of devolution from the powerful administrative state, returning power down to local levels, will almost certainly bear within it the seeds of future protests against itself and the beginnings of yet another *new* reordering of social institutions: "Everything begins in mysticism and ends in politics" (Charles Peguy).

This is not a pessimistic view. To the extent that it is realistic, it probably points to a happy movement toward recurrent balance, in a social system so dynamic that it is always in motion.

At the present moment, the most glaring dysfunction is located in the large, sclerotic welfare state. The creative impulse is located in the people at the grass roots who no longer trust big government. The logic of the past sixty years led to an overpromising, underachieving state. A correction, of course, is both essential and healthy. If the twentieth century unfolded under the sign of the state, pictured as a beneficent mother sheltering her children at her bosom, the twenty-first century is likelier to see a rebirth of the idea of freedom, in communities of men and women eager to practice self-government both in their private and in their public lives.

PART FOUR

The Authors Respond

13

Peter Berger and
Richard John Neuhaus Respond

It will soon be twenty years since we composed the document that forms the focus of this volume. The thought is both alarming and consoling, as is frequently the case with retrospective ruminations. The basic alarm, of course, comes from the intimation of mortality that inevitably accompanies such an exercise. There is also the more mundanely alarming apprehension that, neither of us being policy analysts primarily, we might once again get in over our heads. The consolation in this particular case comes from the recognition that the concept of mediating structures is as relevant today as it was in the 1970s and, what is more, that the political climate today is much more auspicious for realizing at least some of the practical implications of that concept.

In any case, nothing has happened in the intervening period to make us change our minds about the strategic importance of these intermediate institutions in a modern society. The world has changed dramatically in the past two decades, and so have we. What has not changed is the basic configuration of modern society, which pits vast, anonymous, and potentially oppressive megastructures against the vulnerable personal worlds of individuals. Foremost among these megastructures, of course, is the modern state. The oppressive power of the modern state reached its climax in twentieth-century totalitarianism. One of the great mercies of the recent period is that the totalitarian project has ignominiously collapsed, at least for the time being, and that the reasons for this collapse have been widely learned. This does not, alas, imply that the "end of history" has arrived and that democratic capitalism will rule from here to eternity: one must never underestimate the human capacity for forgetfulness and imbecility. Still, the climate for democracy, capitalism, and pluralism has never been better, and with this the opportunities for mediating structures to flourish.

But even the most democratic state has at its disposal awesome power to penetrate and control every nook and cranny of social life. It is virtually unavoidable that this power will recurringly be misused, even if the intentions motivating the exercise of power are morally impeccable. As one of us (Neuhaus) has frequently remarked, the doctrine of original sin is the only Christian doctrine that can be empirically demonstrated without the benefit of faith. The modern welfare state is arguably the most important case of an enormous exercise of power, by and large motivated benignly, yet having developed into an instrument of oppression as well as corruption. Built on the twin foundations of the democratic polity and the market economy, the metastasis of the welfare state has come to threaten both. The democratic polity is endangered by the web of bureaucratic regulation spawned by the welfare state, and the market economy by the astronomic costs of the welfare state. Today the welfare state is in crisis in every industrial democracy. This crisis, painful as it is, provides a new chance for the sort of thinking that the concept of mediating structures suggests.

A Shift to the Right

The original publication of *To Empower People* occurred during the Carter administration, a political era that now seems ages ago. Since then, the center of policy discourse in the United States has shifted markedly to the right. The election of November 1994 has, as it were, ratified that shift. As a result, ideas that might have seemed wildly utopian twenty years ago can now be pronounced in matter-of-fact tones by people considered to be politically moderate. This shift holds for any number of issues and is applicable to the policy implications of the concept of mediating structures. The sort of new thinking that is now politically realistic is well summarized in the chapter by Michael Joyce and William Schambra in this volume. In the 1977 publication, we stated that it was not our aim to dismantle the welfare state and that our policy proposals were not primarily concerned with reducing the costs of government. Today it seems plausible to us to be less cautious on both counts. There are some differences between us on this matter (Neuhaus is prepared to envisage a more thorough dismantling of the welfare state than Berger), but we both agree that a more far-reaching restructuring of social policies than we thought of then is now possible and that, given the federal deficit, it is not practical to think of revenue-neutral policies in this area. The chapter by William Galston shows that the rethinking process is not limited to the Republican side of the aisle.

Right now, America is in an inward-looking mood. In view of what is going on in other parts of the world, this is a very dangerous mood indeed. Inward-looking thinking about social policy is obviously less dangerous than such thinking in other policy areas, but it is regrettable nonetheless. What is happening here is part of a much larger picture. The crisis of the welfare state is very much a reality in Western Europe (where, let it not be forgotten, the welfare state was first conceived), and the debates growing from this crisis are quite similar to the American ones. The contribution by David Green makes this similarity clear. As the American discussion proceeds, we think that it would be useful to pay more attention to the international experience, primarily in the advanced industrial societies but also in some developing or newly industrialized countries where there has been innovative thinking about social policy. Chile comes to mind here, with its radical privatization of the pension system. In addition, some of the burgeoning societies of Southeast Asia are looking for ways to limit the role of government in the delivery of social services from the start. A certain role reversal is not impossible here—the more advanced societies might learn lessons from places like Chile or Malaysia (countries that may benefit from what Thorstein Veblen called the "advantage of coming late"). But that topic is better left to possible future projects.

In recent months, there has been a triumphalist rhetoric in right-of-center circles in this country. This response is understandable, indeed well deserved. It is also a bit exaggerated. Thus we do not, in principle, disagree with Jim Pinkerton's view expressed in his chapter, to the effect that on many of these issues the intellectual argument has been won by our side. In principle, yes—that is, the argument has been won if we imagine an impartial and thoroughly rational audience. Unfortunately, such audiences are rare. Despite all the good arguments that Pinkerton has in mind, the old paradigm of the welfare state continues to haunt the political discourse. It is based on the following formula for social policy: locate a social problem; define it as a government responsibility; set up a government program designed to solve it. Intellectual habits die as slowly as other habits. People who have thought according to this formula for many years are not easily induced to look at reality in new ways. But there is more at stake here than sluggish mind-sets. Very large and powerful vested interests have grown up around every policy of the welfare state. The paradigm shift suggested by the concept of mediating structures directly threatens some of those interests. Needless to say, they will fight back. Indeed, wherever anything resembling the concept has been tried, the resistance has been fierce. One need only mention here the ferocious opposition of the teachers' unions to any educational reform that involves true parental freedom in choosing schools.

The Definition of *Mediating Structures*

The concept of mediating structures was well received fairly widely across the ideological spectrum when we first expounded it. Already then, this reception should have worried us. Soon, the term itself, *mediating structures*, became a household word, frequently cited without quotation marks and without reference to our little book. We did not complain, indeed, felt flattered. It is, after all, gratifying if a word one has coined comes into usage as a common noun—like *coke,* or *xeroxing,* or *fridge.* Perhaps inevitably, though, the quick diffusion of the concept led to serious misinterpretations. Our definition of mediating structures was rather clear: those institutions that stand between the private world of individuals and the large, impersonal structures of modern society. They "mediated" by constituting a vehicle by which personal beliefs and values could be transmitted into the mega-institutions. They were thus "Janus-faced" institutions, facing both "upward" and "downward." Their mediations were then of benefit to both levels of social life: the individual was protected from the alienations and "anomie" of modern life, while the large institutions, including the state, gained legitimacy by being related to values that governed the actual lives of ordinary people. In this definition, mediation is as mediation does. In other words, we did not propose an arbitrary, abstract list of institutions that should properly be called mediating (although we cited some broad categories, such as voluntary association, church, neighborhood). Rather, we suggested that an institution should be considered a mediating structure if indeed it fulfilled a mediating role. This definitional element was misunderstood in interesting ways, both on the Left and on the Right. On the Left, the concept was understood in terms of grass-roots mobilization and, more recently, in communitarian terms. To be sure, some grass-roots organizations and local communities might indeed be mediating structures. But they might not be, either being invasions of people's life worlds by agents from the outside, in which case they are simply branches of mega-institutions, or being enclaves of private meanings and lifestyles with no relation to the larger society. On the Right, the concept was understood as including all institutions outside government, which, of course, stretches the concept beyond any usefulness. Neither General Motors nor the United Methodist Church is a mediating structure, though a workshop within a GM plant might be, as might a local Methodist congregation. As a matter of fact, even a local government agency might have a meaningful relationship with the values of the people it serves. Not every nongovernmental organization is a mediating structure.

While we coined the phrase, the concept was anything but new. The importance of intermediate institutions has been affirmed by many authors in modern political thought, going at least as far back as Edmund Burke's defense of the "small platoons" against the "geometric" abstractions of the French revolutionaries. The same institutions are included in the principle of "subsidiarity" in Roman Catholic thought. And sociological theory has, in different formulations, looked at these institutions as vital to social cohesion—as in Emile Durkheim's view of voluntary groupings that cushion individuals against the pressures of modernity, or in the distinction between *Gesellschaft* and *Gemeinschaft* in German sociology, or in the fascination of the so-called Chicago School with the manifold communities that spring up to provide meaning and belonging to people living in the anonymous vastness of the modern metropolis. We were quite right in placing ourselves in this reputable stream of social thought. Possibly, though, we were a bit carried away in our enthusiasm for these institutions, overlooking the fact that some of them definitely play nefarious roles in society. Thus, strictly speaking in terms of our definition, the Mafia, the Ku Klux Klan, and the local branch of an organization seeking to get the government to negotiate with visiting aliens in UFOs could also be described as mediating structures. They do, indeed, mediate between individuals and the larger society. It just happens that the beliefs and values thus mediated are criminal, immoral, or plain crazy. We would suggest now that there are (to put it plainly) both good and bad mediating structures and that social policy will have to make this differentiation in terms of the values being mediated. If, for instance, educational vouchers should become part of social policy, they should not be negotiable in schools run by criminals or racist fanatics, nor in schools that would seek to indoctrinate children in a patently lunatic world view. Such discrimination obviously creates certain problems, but they are not insuperable. Thus we have no quarrel with Robert Woodson's description of some very admirable institutions working in inner city neighborhoods. But we are also aware of the fact (as he is) that not all such institutions are equally admirable. Happily, regulation against the pathological is needed only at the margins, since people will, with relatively few exceptions, choose what is best for them and their children. (And the public policy bias should always be toward respecting what people think best.)

The Fatal Embrace of Regulation

In looking back to what we wrote then, we must address the problem that has increasingly come to preoccupy us in the intervening years: how to protect mediating structures from the fatal embrace of government regulation. The problem exists even if no tax funds are available to support these institutions; it obviously grows immensely when tax funds are channeled to them—in the name of accountability, equity, or whatever other moral principle is supposed to govern the expenditure of public money. We were aware of this problem at the time, but we would now say that we did not take it seriously enough. Arguably, it has greatly worsened since then. Unless that problem is solved, when such institutions are first "discovered" and then funded by government, the very vitality that originally distinguished the institutions from government agencies is destroyed. Indeed they *become* government agencies under another name. This is not just an eventuality. It has already happened, across the board, in the area of private philanthropy.

In the 1970s, we underestimated the degree of corruption that comes with government funding—not, of course, corruption in the sense of criminal misuse of funds (that is a relatively manageable matter), but the much more insidious corruption in which these institutions reshape themselves to continue as beneficiaries of government largesse. Douglas Besharov provides a very succinct picture of the different mechanisms by which public money can be channeled to mediating structures, and some may be preferable to others. The aforementioned problem exists no matter which mechanism is used. The chapters by Leslie Lenkowsky and Marvin Olasky provide chilling evidence of the degree of corruption at issue here. The deformation of mediating structures by this process of creeping "governmentalization" must be at the center of any rethinking of social policy.

It follows that we must rethink the options we labeled as "maximalist" and "minimalist" at the time. The maximalist option is the use of mediating structures to deliver social services through tax funds; the minimalist option eschews such funding and simply advocates government should leave the mediating structures alone to operate as they choose. The latter option, of course, is the more classically conservative one. The question is not fully resolved in our own minds. And there were differences of opinion within the group of authors for this volume. Thus, Michael Horowitz clearly favors the minimalist option, while Stuart Butler believes that there are ways of reducing the risk of governmental embrace. Be this as it may, it is clear to us that it is not enough to state a preference for the maximalist option (as we did then). This preference would have to be made conditional upon a package of legislative and policy proposals designed to create a protective umbrella over these institutions. The design of such a package is the agenda for a follow-up project we are now considering. If one should finally conclude that such a package is not realizable under present conditions, one will have to fall back on the minimalist position and resolutely draw the necessary political consequences. The choice is far-reaching and should be at the top of the intellectual agenda.

Two additional aspects of this problem should be considered. If we say that such institutions should be protected, we are implying that they *want* to be protected. In fact, however, many are by now quite content with their status as parastatal agencies. They may have been fatally embraced, but they rather enjoy it and have no desire to be freed from it. We are not sure how one liberates people who are happy in their servitude. Another aspect of the problem is the religious one. Many of the mediating structures are, or at least started out as, arms of the churches. As a consequence of the secularist (or *laïciste*) interpretation of the first amendment by the federal courts in the past forty years and more, religiously defined institutions seeking tax funds have been forced to deemphasize or even deny altogether the religious character that originally served as their raison d'être. Thus we now have the absurd spectacle of, say, a Catholic college that receives government support loudly proclaiming that there is really nothing particularly Catholic about the education offered there. The protective umbrella called for by the maximalist option would, therefore, have to be able to accommodate religious institutions that do not want to secularize themselves for the purpose of receiving government funding. Again, this problem is not insuperable. The experience of several European democracies (such as Germany and the Netherlands) would be helpful here. In the American situation there will have to be an agenda involving both legislation and litigation if this problem is to be solved.

Conclusion

As Michael Novak makes clear in his chapter, the role of mediating structures in social policy raises a number of interrelated questions. The present volume cannot pretend to have answered all of them. It will serve its purpose if it pushes the discussion further, clarifies the options, and at least adumbrates some practical directions.

Looking back twenty years later, we take the risk of sounding self-serving when we say that the political culture of 1977 was not as favorable as it is today to the arguments of *To Empower People*. We would emphasize, however, that, unlike some aspects of today's political culture, the mediating structures proposal is not antigovernment. We are favorably disposed toward government. We strongly support the form of government that has marked the American experiment at its best, namely, self-governance. In his encyclical on social doctrine, *Centesimus Annus* (The Hundredth Year), Pope John Paul II presses the concept of the "subjectivity of society." The idea is that persons and persons in community are best situated to answer what Aristotle said is *the* political question: How ought we to order our life together? In this sense, people do need to govern themselves. The "state" does not instruct the people; the people instruct the state.

The political question is also a moral question, and the mediating structures proposal will not go very far unless it engages the intellectual and moral energies of the next generation. In the past fifty years, it is fair to say, intellectual and moral excitement about social policy was largely captive to the governmentalizing of human behavior. It typically assumed that people are not capable of self-governance. There were no doubt many reasons for that captivity. The Great Depression and the nationalizing of energies in World War II were contributing factors. Then, too, the careers of many intellectuals became increasingly dependent on expanding government. But, at a deeper level, there was an intellectual alienation from what might be called the everyday life of Americans. The "little platoons" of family, neighborhood, and church were viewed as outdated, stifling, and "parochial." The new thing, the exciting thing, was planning, rationality, and social redesign—in a word, expanded government control.

Is it possible to generate intellectual excitement about everyday lives of everyday people? Without falling prey to the romantic delusions of some stripes of populism, we think the answer is yes. We very much hope it is possible, for the alternative is an intellectual class as the permanent enemy of a people who are in a state of continuous resentment against those who presume to know better than they how they ought to live their lives. Beyond specific policy directions, *To Empower People* is an invitation to rediscover the intellectual and moral excitement of the American experiment, which is the American people's exploration of their capacity to govern themselves in freedom and in whatever virtue can be mustered in a far from perfect world.

* * *

What remains is to express our appreciation to a number of individuals and institutions: To William Schambra, who first suggested this project. To Michael Novak, for convening the group of authors and leading the meetings that brought them together in Washington. To the American Enterprise Institute, for being host to the meetings and for publishing this volume. To Boston University, for letting its Institute for the Study of Economic Culture (which Berger directs) engage in explorations of a practical nature that social science research centers often shy away from. To the Lynde and Harry Bradley Foundation, which funded the exercise. We are indebted most, of course, to the authors, who have generously given of their time and energy.

PART FIVE

The Original Text

I

Mediating Structures and the Dilemmas of the Welfare State

wo seemingly contradictory tendencies are evident in current thinking about public policy in America. First, there is a continuing desire for the services provided by the modern welfare state. Partisan rhetoric aside, few people seriously envisage dismantling the welfare state. The serious debate is over how and to what extent it should be expanded. The second tendency is one of strong animus against government, bureaucracy, and bigness as such. This animus is directed not only toward Washington but toward government at all levels. Although this essay is addressed to the American situation, it should be noted that a similar ambiguity about the modern welfare state exists in other democratic societies, notably in Western Europe.

Perhaps this is just another case of people wanting to eat their cake and have it too. It would hardly be the first time in history that the people wanted benefits without paying the requisite costs. Nor are politicians above exploiting ambiguities by promising increased services while reducing expenditures. The extravagant rhetoric of the modern state and the surrealistic vastness of its taxation system encourage magical expectations that make contradictory measures seem possible. As long as some of the people can be fooled some of the time, some politicians will continue to ride into office on such magic.

But this is not the whole story. The contradiction between wanting more government services and less government may be only apparent. More precisely, we suggest that the modern welfare state is here to stay, indeed that it ought to expand the benefits it provides—but that *alternative mechanisms are possible to provide welfare-state services.*

The current anti-government, anti-bigness mood is not irrational. Complaints about impersonality, unresponsiveness, and excessive interference, as well as the perception of rising costs and deteriorating service—these are based upon empirical and widespread experience. The crisis of New York City, which is rightly seen as more than a fiscal crisis, signals a national state of unease with the policies followed in recent decades. At the same time there is widespread public support for publicly addressing major problems of our society in relieving poverty, in education, health care, and housing, and in a host of other human needs. What first appears as contradiction, then, is the sum of equally justified aspirations. The public policy goal is to address human needs without exacerbating the reasons for animus against the welfare state.

Of course there are no panaceas. The alternatives proposed here, we believe, can solve *some* problems. Taken seriously, they could become the basis of far-reaching innovations in public policy, perhaps of a new paradigm for at least sectors of the modern welfare state.

The basic concept is that of what we are calling mediating structures. The concept in various forms has been around for a long time. What is new is the systematic effort to translate it into specific public policies. For purposes of this study, mediating structures are defined as *those institutions standing between the individual in his private life and the large institutions of public life.*

Modernization brings about a historically unprecedented dichotomy between public and private life. The most important large institution in the ordering of modern society is the modern state itself. In addition, there are the large economic conglomerates of capitalist enterprise, big labor, and the growing bureaucracies that administer wide sectors of the society, such as in education and the organized professions. All these institutions we call the megastructures.

Then there is that modern phenomenon called private life. It is a curious kind of preserve left over by the large institutions and in which individuals carry on a bewildering variety of activities with only fragile institutional support.

For the individual in modern society, life is an ongoing migration between these two spheres, public and private. The megastructures are typically alienating, that is, they are not helpful in providing meaning and identity for individual existence. Meaning, fulfillment, and personal identity are to be realized in the private sphere. While the two spheres interact in many ways, in private life the individual is left very much to his own devices, and thus is uncertain and anxious. Where modern society is "hard," as in the megastructures, it is personally unsatisfactory; where it is "soft," as in private life, it cannot be relied upon. Compare, for example, the social realities of employment with those of marriage.

The dichotomy poses a double crisis. It is a crisis for the individual who must carry on a balancing act between the demands of the two spheres. It is a political crisis because the megastructures (notably the state) come to be devoid of personal meaning and are therefore viewed as unreal or even malignant. Not everyone experiences this crisis in the same way. Many who handle it more successfully than most have access to institutions that *mediate* between the two spheres. Such institutions have a private face, giving private life a measure of stability, and they have a public face, transferring meaning and value to the megastructures. Thus, mediating structures alleviate each facet of the double crisis of modern society. Their strategic position derives from their reducing both the anomic precariousness of individual existence in isolation from society and the threat of alienation to the public order.

Our focus is on four such mediating structures—neighborhood, family, church, and voluntary association. This is by no means an exhaustive list, but these institutions were selected for two reasons: first, they figure prominently in the lives of most Americans and, second, they are most relevant to the problems of the welfare state with which we are concerned. The proposal is that, if these institutions could be more imaginatively recognized in public policy, individuals would be more "at home" in society, and the political order would be more "meaningful."

Without institutionally reliable processes of mediation, the political order becomes detached from the values and realities of individual life. Deprived of its moral foundation, the political order is "delegitimated." When that happens, the political order must be secured by coercion rather than by consent. And when that happens, democracy disappears.

The attractiveness of totalitarianism—whether instituted under left-wing or right-wing banners—is that it overcomes the dichotomy of private and public existence by imposing on life one comprehensive order of meaning. Although established totalitarian systems can be bitterly disappointing to their architects as well as their subjects, they are, on the historical record, nearly impossible to dismantle. The system continues quite effectively, even if viewed with cynicism by most of the population—including those who are in charge.

Democracy is "handicapped" by being more vulnerable to the erosion of meaning in its institutions. Cynicism threatens it; wholesale cynicism can destroy it. That is why mediation is so crucial to democracy. Such mediation cannot be sporadic and occasional; it must be institutionalized in *structures*. The structures we have chosen to study have demonstrated a great capacity for adapting and innovating under changing conditions. Most important, they exist where people are, and that is where sound public policy should always begin.

This understanding of mediating structures is sympathetic to Edmund Burke's well-known claim: "To be attached to the subdivision, to love the little platoon we belong to in society, is the first principle (the germ as it were) of public affections." And it is sympathetic to Alexis de Tocqueville's conclusion drawn from his observation of Americans: "In democratic countries the science of association is the mother of science; the progress of all the rest depends upon the progress it has made." Marx too was concerned about the destruction of community, and the glimpse he gives us of postrevolutionary society is strongly reminiscent of Burke's "little platoons." The emphasis is even sharper in the anarcho-syndicalist tradition of social thought.

In his classic study of suicide, Emile Durkheim describes the "tempest" of modernization sweeping away the "little aggregations" in which people formerly found community, leaving only the state on the one hand and a mass of individuals, "like so many liquid molecules," on the other. Although using different terminologies, others in the sociological tradition—Ferdinand Toennies, Max Weber, Georg Simmel, Charles Cooley, Thorstein Veblen—have analyzed aspects of the same dilemma. Today Robert Nisbet has most persuasively argued that the loss of community threatens the future of American democracy.

Also, on the practical political level, it might seem that mediating structures have universal endorsement. There is, for example, little political mileage in being anti-family or anti-church. But the reality is not so simple. Liberalism—which constitutes the broad center of American politics, whether or not it calls itself by that name—has tended to be blind to the political (as distinct from private) functions of mediating structures. The main feature of liberalism, as we intend the term, is a commitment to government action toward greater social justice within the existing system. (To revolutionaries, of course, this is "mere reformism," but the revolutionary option has not been especially relevant, to date, in the American context.) Liberalism's blindness to mediating structures can be traced to its Enlightenment roots. Enlightenment thought is abstract, universalistic, addicted to what Burke called "geometry" in social policy. The concrete particularities of mediating structures find an inhospitable soil in the liberal garden. There the great concern is for the individual ("the rights of man") and for a just public order, but anything "in between" is viewed as irrelevant, or even an obstacle, to the rational ordering of society. What lies in between is dismissed, to the extent it can be, as superstition, bigotry, or (more recently) cultural lag.

American liberalism has been vigorous in the defense of the private rights of individuals, and has tended to dismiss the argument that private behavior can have public consequences. Private rights are frequently defended *against* mediating structures— children's rights against the family, the rights of sexual deviants against neighborhood or small-town sentiment, and so forth. Similarly, American liberals are virtually faultless in their commitment to the religious liberty of individuals. But the liberty to be defended is always that of privatized religion. Supported by a very narrow understanding of the separation of church and state, liberals are typically hostile to the claim that institutional religion might have public rights and public functions. As a consequence of this "geometrical" outlook, liberalism has a hard time coming to terms with the alienating effects of the abstract structures it has multiplied since the New Deal. This may be the Achilles heel of the liberal state today.

The left, understood as some version of the socialist vision, has been less blind to the problem of mediation. Indeed the term alienation derives from Marxism. The weakness of the left, however, is its exclusive or nearly exclusive focus on the capitalist economy as the source of this evil, when in fact the alienations of the socialist states, insofar as there are socialist states, are much more severe than those of the capitalist states. While some theorists of the New Left have addressed this problem by using elements from the anarcho-syndicalist tradition, most socialists see mediating structures as something that may be relevant to a postrevolutionary future, but that in the present only distracts attention from the struggle toward building socialism. Thus the left is not very helpful in the search for practical solutions to our problem.

On the right of the political broad center, we also find little that is helpful. To be sure, classical European conservatism had high regard for mediating structures, but, from the eighteenth century on, this tradition has been marred by a romantic urge to revoke modernity—a prospect that is, we think, neither likely nor desirable. On the other hand, what is now called conservatism in America is in fact old-style liberalism. It is the laissez-faire ideology of the period before the New Deal, which is roughly the time when liberalism shifted its faith from the market to government. *Both* the old faith in the market *and* the new faith in government share the abstract thought patterns of the Enlightenment. In addition, today's conservatism typically exhibits the weakness of the left in reverse: it is highly sensitive to the alienations of big government, but blind to the analogous effects of big business. Such one-sidedness, whether left or right, is not helpful.

As is now being widely recognized, we need new approaches free of the ideological baggage of the past. The mediating structures paradigm cuts across current ideological and political divides. This proposal has met with gratifying interest from most with whom we have shared it, and while it has been condemned as right-wing by some and as left-wing by others, this is in fact encouraging. Although the paradigm may play havoc with the conventional political labels, it is hoped that, after the initial confusion of what some social scientists call "cognitive shock," each implication of the proposal will be considered on its own merits.

The argument of this essay—and the focus of the research project it is designed to introduce—can be subsumed under three propositions. The first proposition is analytical: *Mediating struc-*

tures are essential for a vital democratic society. The other two are broad programmatic recommendations: *Public policy should protect and foster mediating structures,* and *Wherever possible, public policy should utilize mediating structures for the realization of social purposes.* The research project will determine, it is hoped, whether these propositions stand up under rigorous examination and, if so, how they can be translated into specific recommendations.

The analytical proposition assumes that mediating structures are the value-generating and value-maintaining agencies in society. Without them, values become another function of the megastructures, notably of the state, and this is a hallmark of totalitarianism. In the totalitarian case, the individual becomes the object rather than the subject of the value-propagating processes of society.

The two programmatic propositions are, respectively, minimalist and maximalist. Minimally, public policy should cease and desist from damaging mediating structures. Much of the damage has been unintentional in the past. We should be more cautious than we have been. As we have learned to ask about the effects of government action upon racial minorities or upon the environment, so we should learn to ask about the effects of public policies on mediating structures.

The maximalist proposition ("utilize mediating structures") is much the riskier. We emphasize, "wherever possible." The mediating structures paradigm is not applicable to all areas of policy. Also, there is the real danger that such structures might be "co-opted" by the government in a too eager embrace that would destroy the very distinctiveness of their function. The prospect of government control of the family, for example, is clearly the exact opposite of our intention. The goal in utilizing mediating structures is to expand government services without producing government oppressiveness. Indeed it might be argued that the achievement of that goal is one of the acid tests of democracy.

It should be noted that these propositions differ from superficially similar proposals aimed at decentralizing governmental functions. Decentralization is limited to what can be done *within* governmental structures; we are concerned with the structures that stand *between* government and the individual. Nor, again, are we calling for a devolution of governmental responsibilities that would be tantamount to dismantling the welfare state. We aim rather at rethinking the institutional means by which government exercises its responsibilities. The idea is not to revoke the New Deal but to pursue its vision in ways more compatible with democratic governance.

Finally, there is a growing ideology based upon the proposition that "small is beautiful." We are sympathetic to that sentiment in some respects, but we do not share its programmatic antagonism to the basic features of modern society. Our point is not to attack the megastructures but to find better ways in which they can relate to the "little platoons" in our common life.

The theme is *empowerment.* One of the most debilitating results of modernization is a feeling of powerlessness in the face of institutions controlled by those whom we do not know and whose values we often do not share. Lest there be any doubt, our belief is that human beings, whoever they are, understand their own needs better than anyone else—in, say, 99 percent of all cases. The mediating structures under discussion here are the principal expressions of the real values and the real needs of people in our society. They are, for the most part, the people-sized institutions. Public policy should recognize, respect, and, where possible, empower these institutions.

A word about the poor is in order. Upper-income people already have ways to resist the encroachment of megastructures. It is not their children who are at the mercy of alleged child experts, not their health which is endangered by miscellaneous vested interests, not their neighborhoods which are made the playthings of utopian planners. Upper-income people may allow themselves to be victimized on all these scores, but they do have ways to resist if they choose to resist. Poor people have this power to a much lesser degree. The paradigm of mediating structures aims at empowering poor people to do the things that the more affluent can already do, aims at spreading the power around a bit more—and to do so where it matters, in people's control over their own lives. Some may call this populism. But that term has been marred by utopianism and by the politics of resentment. We choose to describe it as the empowerment of people.

II

Neighborhood

T he most sensible way to locate the neighborhood," writes Milton
Kotler in *Neighborhood Government* (Bobbs-Merrill, 1969) "is
to ask people where it is, for people spend much time fixing its
boundaries. Gangs mark its turf. Old people watch for its new faces.
Children figure out safe routes between home and school. People
walk their dogs through their neighborhood, but rarely beyond it."

At first blush, it seems the defense of neighborhood is a moth-
erhood issue. The neighborhood is the place of relatively intact and
secure existence, protecting us against the disjointed and threatening big world "out there." Around the idea of neighborhood gravi-
tate warm feelings of nostalgia and the hope for community. It may
not be the place where we are entirely at home, but it is the place
where we are least homeless.

While no doubt influenced by such sentiments, the new interest in neighborhoods today goes far beyond sentimentality. The
neighborhood should be seen as a key mediating structure in the
reordering of our national life. As is evident in fears and confusions
surrounding such phrases as ethnic purity or neighborhood integrity, the focus on neighborhood touches some of the most urgent
and sensitive issues of social policy. Indeed, many charge that
the "rediscovery" of the neighborhood is but another, and thinly
veiled, manifestation of racism.

Against that charge we contend—together with many others,

both black and white, who have a strong record of commitment to racial justice—that strong neighborhoods can be a potent instrument in achieving greater justice for all Americans. It is not true, for example, that all-black neighborhoods are by definition weak neighborhoods. As we shall see, to argue the contrary is to relegate black America to perpetual frustration or to propose a most improbable program of social revolution. To put it simply, real community development must begin where people are. If our hopes for development assume an idealized society cleansed of ethnic pride and its accompanying bigotries, they are doomed to failure.

While social policy that can be morally approved must be attuned to the needs of the poor—and in America that means very particularly the black poor—the nonpoor also live in and cherish the values of neighborhood. The neighborhood in question may be as part-time and tenuous as the many bedroom communities surrounding our major cities; it may be the ethnic and economic crazy-quilt of New York's East Village; it may be the tranquil homogeneity of the east side of Cisco, Texas. Again, a neighborhood is what the people who live there say is a neighborhood.

For public policy purposes, there is no useful definition of what makes a good neighborhood, though we can agree on what constitutes a bad neighborhood. Few people would choose to live where crime is rampant, housing deteriorated, and garbage uncollected. To describe these phenomena as bad is not an instance of imposing middle-class, bourgeois values upon the poor. No one, least of all the poor, is opposed to such "middle class" values as safety, sanitation, and the freedom of choice that comes with affluence. With respect to so-called bad neighborhoods, we have essentially three public policy choices: we can ignore them, we can attempt to dismantle them and spread their problems around more equitably, or we can try to transform the bad into the better on the way to becoming good. The first option, although common, should be intolerable. The second is massively threatening to the nonpoor, and therefore not feasible short of revolution. The third holds most promise for a public policy that can gain the support of the American people. And, if we care more about consequence than about confrontation, the third is also the most radical in long-range effect.

Because social scientists and planners have a penchant for unitary definitions that cover all contingencies, there is still much discussion of what makes for a good neighborhood. Our approach suggests that the penchant should be carefully restrained. It is not necessarily true, for example, that a vital neighborhood is one that supplies a strong sense of social cohesion or reinforces personal identity with the group. In fact many people want neighborhoods where free choice in association and even anonymity are cherished. That kind of neighborhood, usually urban, is no less a neighborhood for its lack of social cohesion. Cohesion exacts its price in loss of personal freedom; freedom may be paid for in the coin of alienation and loneliness. One pays the price for the neighborhood of one's choice. Making that choice possible is the function of the *idea* of neighborhood as it is embodied in many actual neighborhoods. It is not possible to create the benefits of each kind of neighborhood in every neighborhood. One cannot devise a compromise between the cohesion of a New England small town and the anonymity of the East Village without destroying both options.

Nor is it necessarily true that progress is marked by movement from the neighborhood of cohesion to the neighborhood of elective choice. Members of the cultural elite, who have strong influence on the metaphors by which public policy is designed, frequently feel they have escaped from the parochialisms of the former type of neighborhood. Such escapes are one source of the continuing vitality of great cities, but this idea of liberation should not be made normative. The Upper West Side of New York City, for example, the neighborhood of so many literary, academic, and political persons, has its own forms of parochialism, its taboos and restrictions, approved beliefs and behavior patterns. The urban sophisticate's conformity to the values of individual self-fulfillment and tolerance can be as intolerant of the beliefs and behavior nurtured in the community centered in the St. Stanislaus American Legion branch of Hamtramck, Michigan, as the people of Hamtramck are intolerant of what is called liberation on the Upper West Side.

Karl Marx wrote tellingly of "the idiocy of village life." Important to our approach, however, is the recognition that what looks like idiocy may in fact be a kind of complexity with which we cannot cope or do not wish to be bothered. That is, the movement from the community of cohesion to cosmopolitanism, from village to urban neighborhood, is not necessarily a movement from the simple to the complex. In fact, those who move toward the cosmopolitan may be simplifying their lives by freeing themselves from the tangled associations—family, church, club, and so forth—that dominate village life. It is probably easier for an outsider to become a person of political and social consequence in New York City than in most small towns. In a large city almost everyone is an outsider by definition. To put it another way, in the world of urban émigrés there are enough little worlds so that everyone can be an insider somewhere. Against the urban and universalizing biases of much social thought, the mediating structures paradigm requires that we take seriously the structures, values, and habits by which people order their lives in neighborhoods, wherever those neighborhoods may be, and no matter whether they are cohesive or individualistic, elective or hereditary. There is no inherent superiority in or inevitable movement toward the neighborhood whose life gravitates around the liberal Democratic club rather than around the parish church or union hall. The goal of public policy should be to sustain the diversity of neighborhoods in which people can remain and to which they can move in accord with what "fits" their self-understanding and their hopes for those about whom they care most.

The empowerment of people in neighborhoods is hardly the answer to all our social problems. Neighborhoods empowered to impose their values upon individual behavior and expression can be both coercive and cruel. Government that transcends neighborhoods must intervene to protect elementary human rights. Here again, however, the distinction between public and private spheres is critically important. In recent years an unbalanced emphasis upon individual rights has seriously eroded the community's power to sustain its democratically determined values in the public sphere. It is ironic, for example, to find people who support landmark commissions that exercise aesthetic censorship—for example, by forbidding owners of landmark properties to change so much as a step or a bay window without legal permission and who, at the same time, oppose public control of pornography, prostitution, gambling, and other "victimless crimes" that violate neighborhood values more basic than mere aesthetics. In truth, a strong class factor is involved in this apparent contradiction. Houses in neighborhoods that are thought to be part of our architectural heritage are typically owned by people to whom values such as architectural heritage are important. These are usually not the people whose neighborhoods are assaulted by pornography, prostitution, and drug trafficking. In short, those who have power can call in the police to reinforce their values while the less powerful cannot.

This individualistic and neighborhood-destroying bias is reinforced by court judgments that tend to treat all neighborhoods alike. That is, the legal tendency is to assume that there is a unitary national community rather than a national community composed of thousands of communities. Thus, the people of Kokomo, Indiana, must accept public promotions of pornography, for instance, because such promotions are protected by precedents established in Berkeley, California, or in Times Square. It is just barely arguable that the person who wants to see a live sex show in downtown Kokomo would be denied a constitutional right were such shows locally prohibited. It is a great deal clearer that the people of Kokomo are now denied the right to determine democratically the character of the community in which they live. More careful distinctions are required if we are to stay the rush toward a situation in which civil liberties are viewed as the enemy of communal values and law itself is pitted against the power of people to shape their own lives. Such distinctions must reflect a greater appreciation of the differences between public and private behavior.

One reason for the present confusion about individual and communal rights has been the unreflective extension of policies deriving from America's racial dilemma to other areas where they are neither practicable nor just. That is, as a nation, and after a long, tortuous, and continuing agony, we have solemnly covenanted to disallow any public regulation that discriminates on the basis of race. That national decision must in no way be compromised. At the same time, the singularity of America's racial history needs to be underscored. Public policy should be discriminating about discriminations. Discrimination is the essence of particularism and particularism is the essence of pluralism. The careless expansion of antidiscrimination rulings in order to appease every aggrieved minority or individual will have two certain consequences: first, it will further erode local communal authority and, second, it will trivialize the historic grievances and claims to justice of America's racial minorities.

In terms of communal standards and sanctions, deviance always exacts a price. Indeed, without such standards, there can be no such thing as deviance. Someone who engages in public and deviant behavior in, say, Paducah, Kentucky, can pay the social price of deviance, can persuade his fellow citizens to accept his behavior, or can move to New York City. He should not be able to call in the police to prevent the people of Paducah from enforcing their values against his behavior. (Obviously, we are not referring to the expression of unpopular political or religious views, which, like proscriptions against racial discrimination, is firmly protected by national law and consensus.) The city—variously viewed as the cesspool of wickedness or the zone of liberation—has historically been the place of refuge for the insistently deviant. It might be objected that our saying "he can move to the city" sounds like the "love it or leave it" argument of those who opposed anti-war protesters in the last decade. The whole point, however, is the dramatic difference between a nation and a neighborhood. One is a citizen of a nation and lays claim to the rights by which that nation is constituted. Within that nation there are numerous associations such as neighborhoods more or less freely chosen—and membership in those associations is usually related to affinity. This nation is constituted as an exercise in pluralism, as the *unum* within which myriad *plures* are sustained. If it becomes national policy to make the public values of Kokomo or Salt Lake City indistinguishable from those of San Francisco or New Orleans, we have as a nation abandoned the social experiment symbolized by the phrase "E Pluribus Unum."

Viewed in this light, the *national* purpose does not destroy but aims at strengthening particularity, including the particularity of the neighborhood. It would be naive, however, to deny that there are points at which the *unum* and the *plures* are in conflict. It is patently the case, for example, that one of the chief determinants in shaping neighborhoods, especially in urban areas, is the racism that marks American life. The problem, of course, is that racial discrimination is often inseparable from other discriminations based upon attitudes, behavior patterns, and economic disparities. One may sympathize with those who are so frustrated in their effort to overcome racial injustice that they advocate policies aimed at wiping out every vestige and consequence of past racial discrimination. In fact, however, such leveling policies are relentlessly resisted by almost all Americans, including the black and the poor who, rightly or wrongly, see their interests attached to a system of rewards roughly associated with "free enterprise." The more practicable and, finally, the more just course is advanced by those who advocate massive public policy support for neighborhood development as development is defined by the people in the neighborhoods. As people in poor neighborhoods realize more of the "middle class" goals to which they undoubtedly aspire, racial discrimination will be reduced or at least will be more readily isolated than now and thus more easily reachable by legal proscription. The achievement of the poor need not mean that achievers move out of poor neighborhoods, thus leaving behind a hard core of more "ghettoized" residents. It is often overlooked, for example, that many middle-class and wealthy blacks *choose* to live in Harlem, creating "good neighborhoods" within an area often dismissed as hopeless. The dynamics of such community maintenance deserve more careful study and wider appreciation.

The pervasiveness of racial prejudice among whites means that blacks cannot depend upon economic mobility alone to gain freedom in choosing where to live and how to live. The communications media, churches, schools, government, and other institutions with some moral authority must continue and indeed intensify efforts to educate against racial bias. Where instances of racial discrimination can be reasonably isolated from other factors, they must be rigorously prosecuted and punished. It remains true, however, that economics and the values associated with middle-class status are key to overcoming racism. The public policy focus must therefore be on the development of the communities where people are. To the objection that this means locking the black and poor into present patterns of segregation, it must be answered that nothing would so surely lock millions of black Americans into hopelessness as making progress contingent upon a revolution in American racial attitudes or in the economic system. It is not too much to say that the alternative to neighborhood development is either neglect or revolution. Neglect is morally intolerable and, in the long run, probably too costly to the whole society to be viable even if it were acceptable morally. Revolution is so utterly improbable that it would be an unconscionable cruelty to encourage the poor to count on it.

The current attack on the existing pattern of housing and zoning regulations is, we believe, wrongheaded in several respects. Unless such regulations are almost totally dismantled, the attack is hardly worth pressing; and, if they are dismantled, the likely result would be great injustice to the poor whom the changes were designed to benefit and to the nonpoor who would certainly resist such changes. Those who propose to overcome poverty by spreading the poor more evenly seldom consider whether the burden of poverty might not be increased by virtue of its stark contrast with the affluence it would then be forced to live with. Even were it logistically and politically possible to distribute South Chicago's welfare families throughout the metropolitan area, it is doubtful their lot would be improved by living in projects, large or small, next to the $80,000 homes of the more prosperous suburbs. The people who live in those suburbs now do so quite deliberately in order to get away from the social problems associated with poverty—and, in a fashion too often related to racism, to get away from the minorities most commonly associated with those problems. It is one thing to make white Americans feel guilty about racism; it is quite another (and both wrong and futile) to make them feel guilty about their middle-class values—values also enthusiastically endorsed by the poor. These considerations aside, the great wrong in proposals to overcome poverty by dispersing the poor is that they would deprive the poor, whether black or white, of their own communities. Again, the proposition implicit in so much well-intended social advocacy—the proposition that an all-black neighborhood or all-black school is of necessity inferior—is aptly described as reverse racism. To the extent the proposition is internalized by the black poor, it also tends to become a self-fulfilling prophecy.

In sum, with respect to the connection between neighborhood and race, we would draw a sharp distinction between a society of *pro*scription and a society of *pre*scription. We have as a society covenanted to proscribe racial discrimination in the public realm. That proscription must be tirelessly implemented, no matter how frustrating the efforts at implementation sometimes are. But it is quite another matter to pursue policies of prescription in which government agencies prescribe quotas and balances for the redistribution of people and wealth. Pushed far enough, the second course invites revolutionary reaction, and it would almost certainly be revolution from the right. Pushed as far as it is now being pushed, it is eroding community power, distracting from the tasks of neighborhood development, and alienating many Americans from the general direction of domestic public policy.

If it is to make a real difference, neighborhood development should be distinguished from programs of decentralization. From Honolulu to Newton, Massachusetts, the last ten years have witnessed an explosion of neighborhood councils, "little city halls" dispersed through urban areas, and the like. Again, the decentralized operation of megastructures is not the same thing as the creation of vital mediating structures—indeed, it can be quite the opposite. Decentralization can give the people in the neighborhoods the feeling that they are being listened to, and even participating, but it has little to do with development and governance unless it means the reality as well as the sensations of power. Neighborhood governance exists when—in areas such as education, health services, law enforcement, and housing regulation—the people democratically determine what is in the interest of their own chosen life styles and values.

Many different streams flow into the current enthusiasms for neighborhood government. Sometimes the neighborhood government movement is dubbed "the new Jeffersonianism." After two centuries of massive immigration and urbanization, we cannot share Jefferson's bucolic vision of rural and small-town America, just as we do not indulge the re-medievalizing fantasies associated in some quarters with the acclaim for smallness. We believe the premise on which to devise public policy is that the parameters of modern, industrial, technological society are set for the foreseeable future. Our argument is not against modernity but in favor of exploring the ways in which modernity can be made more humane. With respect to neighborhood government, for example, it was widely assumed fifty and more years ago that modernity required the "rationalization" of urban polity. This was the premise of the "reform" and "good government" movements promoting the managerial, as distinct from partisan political, style of urban governance. The limitations of that approach are more widely recognized today.

It is recognized, for example, that the managerial model, however well-intended in many instances, served certain vested interests. Black writers and politicians have noted, and with some justice, an apparent racial component in the movement away from what some consider the irrationalities of local control. As urban populations become more black, some reformers put more emphasis upon regional planning and control, thus depriving blacks of their turn at wielding urban power. In 1976, during New York City's fiscal crisis, when more and more power was transferred to the state government, to the banks, and to Washington, it was widely and ruefully remarked that the power brokers were getting ready for the election of the first black or Puerto Rican mayor, who would be endowed with full authority to cut ceremonial ribbons.

In addition, there are today hundreds of thousands of public employees, politicians, planners, and theorists who have deep vested interest in maintaining the dike of "national organization" against what they allege is the threatening chaos of community control. The prospect of neighborhood government must be made to seem less threatening to these many dependents of centralization. Their legitimate interests must be accommodated if neighborhood government is to mature from a protest movement to a guiding metaphor of public policy. A distinction should be made, for example, between unionized professionals and professional unionists. The former need not be threatened by the role we propose for the neighborhood and other mediating structures in public policy. In fact many new opportunities might be opened for the exercise of truly professional imagination in greater responsiveness to the felt needs of people. With many more institutional players in the public realm, professionals could have greater choice and freedom for innovation. The protection of professional interests through unions and other associations need not be dependent upon the perpetuation of the monolithic managerial models for ordering society.

One factor sparking enthusiasm for community control and neighborhood government is the growing realization that localities may not be receiving a fair break when it comes to tax monies. That is, some studies suggest that even poor neighborhoods, after everything is taken into account, end up sending considerably more out of the neighborhood in taxes than is returned. We do not suggest that the income tax, for instance, should be administered locally. It is reasonable to inquire, however, whether the tax-collecting function of the federal and state governments could not be maintained, while the spending function is changed to allow tax monies to be returned in a noncategorical way to the places where they were raised to begin with. Needless to say, this suggestion goes far beyond what is currently called revenue sharing. Nor does it ignore the fact that sizable funds are required for functions that transcend the purview of any neighborhood, such as transportation or defense. But again—focusing on activities of the kind carried on by the Department of Health, Education and Welfare (HEW)—it does imply that the people in communities know best what is needed for the maintenance and development of those communities.

If neighborhoods are to be key to public policy, governmental action is necessary to fund neighborhood improvement. As is well known, practices such as red-lining deteriorating neighborhoods are today very common. It may be that there is no effective way to force private financial institutions to make monies available for home improvement and other investments in "ghetto" neighborhoods. Without a direct assault upon the free enterprise system, the possibilities of evasion and subterfuge in order to invest money where it is safest or most profitable are almost infinite. To strengthen the mediating role of neighborhoods we need to look to new versions of the Federal Housing Administration assistance programs that played such a large part in the burgeoning suburbs after World War II. Such programs can, we believe, be developed to sustain and rehabilitate old communities, as they have been used to build new ones. The idea of urban homesteading, for example, although afflicted with corruption and confusion in recent years, is a move in the right direction. At a very elementary level, property tax regulations should be changed to encourage rather than discourage home improvement. Especially in large metropolitan areas, granting the most generous tax "breaks" might in the not-so-long run yield more revenue than the current system, especially since in many places the abandonment of buildings means that present taxation levels yield little. In short, the tax structure should be changed in every way that encourages the tenant to become a homeowner and the landlord to improve his property.

Neighborhoods will also be strengthened as people in the neighborhood assume more and more responsibility for law enforcement, especially in the effort to stem the tide of criminal terrorism. In this area, too, we have become so enamored of professionalism and so fearful of vigilantism that we have forgotten that community values are only operative when the people in the community act upon them. We should not limit ourselves to thinking about how communities might control conventional police operations and personnel. Rather, we should examine the informal "law enforcement agents" that exist in every community—the woman who runs the local candy store, the people who walk their dogs, or the old people who sit on park benches or observe the streets from their windows. This means new approaches to designing "defensible space" in housing, schools, and the like. It certainly suggests the need to explore the part-time employment, through public funding, of parents and others who would police schools and other public spaces. We have been increasingly impressed, in conversation with people knowledgeable about law enforcement, with the point that there are probably few fields of law enforcement requiring the kind of metropolitan, comprehensive, and professional police force which have come to be taken for granted as an urban necessity. The fact is that there is probably no neighborhood in which the overwhelming majority of residents do not wish to see the laws enforced. Yet the residents feel impotent and therefore the neighborhoods often are impotent in doing anything about crime. The ways in which public policies have fostered that feeling of impotence must be examined, and alternatives to such policies found.

Finally, no discussion of neighborhood can ignore the homogenizing role of the mass communications media in creating a common culture. We suspect, and frankly hope, that the influence of the mass media in destroying the particularisms of American society is frequently overestimated. Television certainly is a tremendous force in creating something like a national discourse regarding current affairs and even values. We do not advocate the dismantling of the national networks. We do propose, however, that it be public policy to open up many unused channels, now technically available, for the use of regional, ethnic, and elective groups of all sorts. Similarly, taxation policies, postal regulations, and other factors should be reexamined with a view toward sustaining neighborhood newspapers and other publications.

All of which is to say that the goal of making and keeping life human, of sustaining a people-sized society, depends upon our learning again that parochialism is not a nasty word. Like the word parish, it comes from the Greek, *para* plus *oikos,* the place next door. Because we all want some choice and all have a great stake in the place where we live, it is in the common interest to empower our own places and the places next door.

III

Family

There are places, especially in urban areas, where life styles are largely detached from family connections. This is, one hopes, good for those who choose it. Certainly such life styles add to the diversity, the creativity, even the magic, of the city. But since a relatively small number of people inhabit these areas, it would be both foolish and undemocratic to take such life styles as guidelines for the nation. For most Americans, neighborhood and community are closely linked to the family as an institution.

The family may be in crisis in the sense that it is undergoing major changes of definition, but there is little evidence that it is in decline. High divorce rates, for example, may indicate not decline but rising expectations in what people look for in marriage and family life. The point is underscored by high remarriage rates. It is noteworthy that the counterculture, which is so critical of the so-called bourgeois family, uses the terminology of family for its new social constructions, as do radical feminists pledged to "sisterhood." For most Americans, the evidence is that involvement in the bourgeois family, however modified, will endure.

Of course, modernization has already had a major impact on the family. It has largely stripped the family of earlier functions in the areas of education and economics, for example. But in other ways, modernization has made the family more important than ever before. It is the major institution within the private sphere, and thus for many people the most valuable thing in their lives. Here they make their moral commitments, invest their emotions, plan for the future, and perhaps even hope for immortality.

There is a paradox here. On the one hand, the megastructures of government, business, mass communications, and the rest have left room for the family to be the autonomous realm of individual aspiration and fulfillment. This room is by now well secured in the legal definitions of the family. At the same time, the megastructures persistently infringe upon the family. We cannot and should not eliminate these infringements entirely. After all, families exist in a common society. We can, however, take positive measures to protect and foster the family institution, so that it is not defenseless before the forces of modernity.

This means public recognition of the family *as an institution*. It is not enough to be concerned for individuals more or less incidentally related to the family as institution. Public recognition of the family as an institution is imperative because every society has an inescapable interest in how children are raised, how values are transmitted to the next generation. Totalitarian regimes have tried—unsuccessfully to date—to supplant the family in this function. Democratic societies dare not try if they wish to remain democratic. Indeed they must resist every step, however well intended, to displace or weaken the family institution.

Public concern for the family is not antagonistic to concern for individual rights. On the contrary, individuals need strong families if they are to grow up and remain rooted in a strong sense of identity and values. Weak families produce uprooted individuals, unsure of their direction and therefore searching for some authority. They are ideal recruits for authoritarian movements inimical to democratic society.

Commitment to the family institution can be combined, although not without difficulty, with an emphatically libertarian view that protects the private lives of adults against public interference of any kind. Public interest in the family is centered on children, not adults; it touches adults insofar as they are in charge of children. The public interest is institutional in character. That is, the state is to view children as members of a family. The sovereignty of the family over children has limits—as does any sovereignty in the modern world—and these limits are already defined in laws regarding abuse, criminal neglect, and so on. The onus of proof, however, must be placed on policies or laws that foster state interference rather than on those that protect family autonomy. In saying this we affirm what has been the major legal tradition in this country.

Conversely, we oppose policies that expose the child directly to state intervention, without the mediation of the family. We are skeptical about much current discussion of children's rights—especially when such rights are asserted *against* the family. Children do have rights, among which is the right to a functionally strong family. When the rhetoric of children's rights means transferring children from the charge of families to the charge of coteries of experts ("We know what is best for the children"), that rhetoric must be suspected of cloaking vested interests—ideological interests, to be sure, but, also and more crudely, interest in jobs, money, and power.

Our preference for the parents over the experts is more than a matter of democratic conviction—and does not ignore the existence of relevant and helpful expertise. It is a bias based upon the simple, but often overlooked, consideration that virtually all parents love their children. Very few experts love, or can love, most of the children in their care. Not only is that emotionally difficult, but expertise generally requires a degree of emotional detachment. In addition, the parent, unlike the expert, has a long-term, open-ended commitment to the individual child. Thus the parent, almost by definition, is way ahead of the expert in sheer knowledge of the child's character, history, and needs. The expert, again by definition, relates to the child within general and abstract schemata. Sometimes the schemata fit, but very often they do not.

We have no intention of glorifying the bourgeois family. Foster parents, lesbians and gays, liberated families, or whatever—all can do the job *as long as* they provide children the loving and the permanent structure that traditional families have typically provided. Indeed, virtually any structure is better for children than what experts or the state can provide.

Most modern societies have in large part disfranchised the family in the key area of education. The family becomes, at best, an auxiliary agency to the state, which at age five or six coercively (compulsory school laws) and monopolistically (for the most part) takes over the child's education. Of course there are private schools, but here class becomes a powerful factor. Disfranchisement falls most heavily on lower-income parents who have little say in what happens to their children in school. This discrimination violates a fundamental human right, perhaps the most fundamental human right—the right to make a world for one's children.

Our purpose is not to deprive upper-income families of the choices they have. The current assault on private schools in Britain (there called public schools) is not a happy example. Our purpose is to give those choices to those who do not now have decision-making power. When some are freezing while others enjoy bright fires, the solution is not to extinguish all fires equally but to provide fires for those who have none.

There is yet a further class discrimination in education. By birth or social mobility, the personnel of the education establishment are upper middle class, and this is reflected in the norms, the procedures, and the very cultural climate of that establishment. This means the child who is not of an upper-middle-class family is confronted by an alien milieu from his or her first day at school. In part this may be inevitable. The modern world is bourgeois and to succeed in a bourgeois world means acquiring bourgeois skills and behavior patterns. We do not suggest, as some do, that the lower-class child is being culturally raped when taught correct English. But there are many other, sometimes unconscious, ways in which the education establishment systematically disparages ways of life other than those of the upper middle class. Yet these disparaged ways of life are precisely the ways in which parents of millions of American children live. Thus schools teach contempt for the parents and, ultimately, self-contempt.

In a few metropolitan areas, the education establishment has responded to these problems, sometimes creatively. But monopolies endowed with coercive powers do not change easily. The best way to induce change is to start breaking up the monopoly—to empower people to *shop elsewhere*. We trust the ability of low-income parents to make educational decisions more wisely than do the professionals who now control their children's education. To deny this ability is the worst class bias of all, and in many instances it is racism as well.

To affirm empowerment against tutelage, irrespective of economic or social status, is hardly a wildly radical position. That it may seem so to some is a measure of the elitist and essentially antidemocratic effects of the bureaucratization and professionalization of American society.

Against the politics of resentment, empowerment is not a zero-sum game. That is, lower-income people can be enfranchised without disfranchising or impoverishing the better off. But this process does assume a lower limit of poverty beyond which efforts at empowerment are futile. Any humane and effective social policy must place a floor of decency under everyone in the society. The relative merits of income maintenance programs—guaranteed income, negative income tax, and so forth—are beyond the scope of this essay, but the whole argument assumes that a floor of decency must be established. Aside from moral imperatives, such a floor can strengthen mediating structures, notably here poor families, by helping them break out of present patterns of dependency upon a confused and confusing welfare system.

The implications of our policy concept may be clarified by looking briefly at three currently discussed issues—education vouchers, day care, and the care of the handicapped. The idea of education vouchers has been around for a while and has had its ups and downs, but it remains one of the most intriguing possibilities for radical reform in the area of education. In this proposal, public funding of education shifts from disbursement to schools to disbursement to individuals. Parents (or, at a certain age, their children) choose the schools where they will cash in their vouchers, the schools then being reimbursed by the state. Essentially the proposal applies the paradigm of the GI Bill to younger students at earlier periods of education. This proposal would break the coercive monopoly of the present education system and empower individuals in relating to the megastructures of bureaucracy and professionalism, with special benefits going to lower-income people. In addition, it would enhance the diversity of American life by fostering particularist communities of value—whether of life style, ideology, religion, or ethnicity. And all this without increasing, and maybe decreasing, costs to the taxpayer since, at least at the primary levels of education, the evidence suggests that economies of scale do not operate.

Politically, education vouchers have advocates on the right and on the left, notably Milton Friedman and Christopher Jencks, respectively. The chief difference is whether vouchers should be basic or total—that is, whether upper-income parents should have the right to supplement vouchers with their own money. Friedman says they should because they have a right to the benefits of their taxes without surrendering the free use of their income. Jencks, for egalitarian reasons, says they should not. On this we incline toward Friedman's position for two reasons: first, the purpose of schools is to educate children, not to equalize income; and second, as stated before, lower-income people can be empowered without penalizing others. Needless to say, the second consideration has much to do with the political salability of education vouchers and, indeed, of the mediating structures paradigm in other policy areas.

There have been limited experiments with the voucher idea within existing public school systems (Seattle; Alum Rock, California; and Gary, Indiana). The results are still being analyzed, but already certain cautions have been raised. An urgent caution is that under no circumstances should vouchers be used to subsidize schools that practice racial exclusion. Another caution is that vouchers are not given a fair trial unless the experiment includes schools outside the public school system. (Of course this raises certain church-state considerations, and we will address them in the next section.)

Among other questions still unanswered: Should vouchers be uniform or graded by income? Should the state insist on a core curriculum, and, if so, should compliancy be ensured by inspection or by examination? Should present methods of teacher certification be extended to schools now considered private? What are the other implications of, in effect, making all schools public schools? And, of course, what would be the effect of a voucher system on teachers unions? Although the unions have tended to be antagonistic to the idea so far, we believe that both bread-and-butter interests and professional interests can be secured, and in some ways better secured than now, within a voucher framework.

Obviously we cannot address all these questions here. We are struck, however, by the fact that almost all the objections to the voucher idea have been on grounds *other than educational.* And education, after all, is what schools are supposed to be about.

Turning to our second example, we note that day care has become a public issue, as more and more mothers of small children have entered the labor force and as many people, spurred by the feminist movement, have begun to claim that working mothers have a right to public services designed to meet their special needs. Both factors are likely to continue, making day care a public issue for the foreseeable future.

Three positions on national day-care policy can be discerned at present. One is that the government should, quite simply, stay out of this area. Financially, it is said, any program will be enormously costly and, ideologically, the government should refrain from intruding itself so massively into the area of early childhood. Another position endorses a federally funded, comprehensive child-care system attached to the public schools. This is the view of the American Federation of Teachers. A third position is much like the second, except that the national program would be less closely linked to the public school system. (This position was embodied in the Mondale-Brademas bill which President Ford vetoed in 1976.) As in the Head Start program, this plan would work through prime sponsors. These sponsors could be private or public, voluntary associations, neighborhood groups, or simply parents getting together to run a day-care center—the only condition being that sponsors be nonprofit in character.

It should come as no surprise that we favor the third position. We do so because there is a real need and because the need should be met in a way that is as inexpensive and as unintrusive as possible. The mediating structures concept is ideally suited to the latter purpose and may also advance the former. As to the second position mentioned above, we are sympathetic to the teachers union's desire for new jobs in a period of educational retrenchment. But, again, providing jobs should not be the purpose of education and child care.

The voucher approach can be the more readily used in day care since there are not as yet in this area the powerful vested interests so firmly established in primary and secondary education. Vouchers would facilitate day-care centers that are small, not professionalized, under the control of parents, and therefore highly diversified. State intervention should be strictly limited to financial accountability and to safety and health standards (which, perhaps not incidentally, are absurdly unrealistic in many states). Considerable funds can be saved through this approach since it is virtually certain that economies of scale do not apply to day-care centers. Imaginative proposals should be explored, such as the use of surrogate grandparents—which, incidentally, would offer meaningful employment to the growing numbers of elderly persons in our society. (We realize that we argued above that employment should not be the purpose of education, but presumably teachers *can* do something other than teach school, while surrogate grandparents may be restricted to grandparenting.)

The third issue mentioned is care of the handicapped. An important case in this area is the so-called special child—special children being those who, for a broad range of nonphysical reasons, are handicapped in their educational development. The field of special education has grown rapidly in recent years and many of its problems (medical and educational as well as legal) are outside our present scope. One problem within our scope is the recurring choice between institutionalizing the severely handicapped and dealing with their problems within the family setting.

Apart from the inability of the normal family to deal with some severe handicaps, the trend toward institutionalization has been propelled by considerations such as the convenience of parents, the vested interests of professionals, and the alleged therapeutic superiority of institutional settings. Because the therapeutic claims of these institutions have been shown to be highly doubtful, and because institutional care is immensely expensive, innovative thinking today moves toward using the family as a therapeutic context *as much as possible*. This means viewing the professional as *ancillary* to, rather than as a substitute for, the resources of the family. It may mean paying families to care for a handicapped child, enabling a parent to work less or not at all, or to employ others. Such an approach would almost certainly reduce costs in caring for the handicapped. More important, and this can be amply demonstrated, the best therapeutic results are obtained when children remain in their families—or, significantly, in institutional settings that imitate family life. (We will not repeat what we said earlier about the relative merits of love and expertise.) And, of course, there is no reason why this proposal could not be extended to the care of handicapped adults.

Again, we are well aware of current misgivings about the traditional family, misgivings pressed by feminists but not by feminists alone. As far as adults are concerned, we favor maximizing choices about life styles. The principal public policy interest in the family concerns children, not adults. This interest is common to all societies, but in democratic society there is an additional and urgent interest in fostering socialization patterns and values that allow individual autonomy. That interest implies enhanced protection of the family in relation to the state, and it implies trusting people to be responsible for their own children in a world of their own making.

IV

Church

R eligious institutions form by far the largest network of voluntary associations in American society. Yet, for reasons both ideological and historical, their role is frequently belittled or totally
overlooked in discussions of social policy. Whatever may be one's
attitude to organized religion, this blind spot must be reckoned a
serious weakness in much thinking about public policy. The churches
and synagogues of America can no more be omitted from responsible
social analysis than can big labor, business corporations, or the communications media. Not only are religious institutions significant
"players" in the public realm, but they are singularly important to
the way people order their lives and values at the most local and
concrete levels of their existence. Thus they are crucial to understanding family, neighborhood, and other mediating structures of
empowerment.

The view that the public sphere is synonymous with the government or the formal polity of the society has been especially effective in excluding religion from considerations of public policy. We
shall return to some of the church/state controversies that have reflected and perpetuated this view; but for the moment it should be
obvious that our whole proposal aims at a complex and nuanced
understanding of the public realm that includes many "players" other
than the state. Also, much modern social thought deriving from Enlightenment traditions has operated on one or two assumptions that
tend to minimize the role of religion. The first assumption is that

education and modernization make certain the decline of allegiance to institutional religion. That is, there is thought to be an inevitable connection between modernization and secularization. The second assumption is that, even if religion continues to flourish, it deals purely with the private sphere of life and is therefore irrelevant to public policy. Both assumptions need to be carefully reexamined.

The evidence, at least in America, does not support the hypothesis of the inevitable decline of religion. Although the decline is perennially announced—its announcement being greeted with both cheers and lamentations—it is likely that religion is at least as institutionally intact as some other major institutions (such as, for example, higher education). It is worth noting that in recent years the alleged decline of religion has been measured by comparison with the so-called religious boom of the late 1950s. The comparison with that unprecedented period of institutional growth offers a very skewed perspective. But, even when the vitality of religion is measured by that misleading comparison, it is notable that in the past few years the indexes are again on the upswing. Church attendance, claimed affiliation, financial contributions, and other indicators all suggest that whatever decline there was from the apex of the late 1950s has now stopped or been reversed. It is perhaps relevant to understanding American society to note that on any given Sunday there are probably more people in churches than the total number of people who attend professional sports events in a whole year—or to note that there are close to 500,000 local churches and synagogues voluntarily supported by the American people.

This is not the place for a detailed discussion of various secularization theories. We are keenly aware of the need to distinguish between institutions of religion and the dynamic of religion as such in society. Let it suffice that our approach raises a strong challenge to the first assumption mentioned above, namely, that in the modern world allegiance to institutional religion must perforce decline. Public policies based upon that highly questionable, if not patently false, assumption will continue to be alienated from one of the most vital dimensions in the lives of many millions of Americans.

The second assumption—that religion deals purely with the private sphere and is therefore irrelevant to public policy—must also be challenged. Although specifically religious activities have been largely privatized, the first part of the proposition overlooks the complex ways in which essentially religious values infiltrate and influence our public thought. But even to the extent that the first part of the proposition is true, it does not follow that religion is therefore irrelevant to public policy. The family, for example, is intimately involved in the institution of religion, and since the family is one of the prime mediating structures (perhaps the prime one), this makes the church urgently relevant to public policy. Without falling into the trap of politicizing all of life, our point is that structures such as family, church, and neighborhood are all public institutions in the sense that they must be taken seriously in the ordering of the polity.

The church (here meaning all institutions of religion) is important not only to the family but also to families and individuals in neighborhoods and other associations. For example, the black community, both historically and at present, cannot be understood apart from the black church. Similarly, the much discussed ethnic community is in large part religiously defined, as are significant parts of American Jewry (sometimes, but not always, subsumed under the phenomenon of ethnicity). And of course the role of religion in small towns or rural communities needs no elaboration. In none of these instances should the religious influence be viewed as residual. Few institutions have demonstrated and continue to demonstrate perduring power comparable to that of religion. It seems that influence is residual only to the extent that the bias of secularizing culture and politics is determined to act as though it is residual. Again, these observations seem to us to be true quite apart from what we may or may not *wish* the influence of religion to be in American society. We are convinced that there is a profoundly antidemocratic prejudice in public policy discourse that ignores the role of religious institutions in the lives of most Americans.

In the public policy areas most relevant to this discussion—health, social welfare, education, and so on—the historical development of programs, ideas, and institutions is inseparable from the church. In some parts of the country, notably in the older cities of the Northeast, the great bulk of social welfare services function under religious auspices. For reasons to be discussed further in the next section, the religious character of these service agencies is being fast eroded. Where government agencies are not directly taking over areas previously serviced by religious institutions, such institutions are being turned into quasi-governmental agencies through the powers of funding, certification, licensing, and the like. The loss of religious and cultural distinctiveness is abetted also by the dynamics of professionalization within the religious institutions and by the failure of the churches either to support their agencies or to insist that public policy respect their distinctiveness. The corollary to the proposition that government responsibilities must be governmentally implemented—a proposition we challenge—is that public is the opposite of sectarian. In public policy discourse sectarian is usually used as a term of opprobrium for anything religious. We contend that this usage and the biases that support it undermine the celebration of distinctiveness essential to social pluralism.

The homogenizing consequences of present patterns of funding, licensing, and certification are intensified by tax policies that have a "chilling effect" upon the readiness of religious institutions to play their part in the public realm. The threatened loss of tax exemption because of excessive "political activity" is a case in point. Even more ominous is the developing notion of tax expenditures (on which more in Section V). Most recently what has been called tax reform has aimed at driving a wedge between churches as such and their church-related auxiliaries, making the latter subject to disclosure, accountability, and therefore greater control by the state. These directions are, we believe, fundamentally wrongheaded. Pushed far enough, they will likely provoke strong reaction from a public that will not countenance what is perceived as an attack on religion. But public policy decision makers should not wait for that reaction to supply a corrective to present tendencies. It is precisely in the interest of public policy to advance a positive approach to the church as a key mediating structure.

Obviously all these questions touch on the complex of issues associated with separation of church and state. We believe, together with many scholars of jurisprudence, that the legal situation of church/state questions is today bogged down in conceptual confusions and practical contradictions. "The wall of separation between church and state" (Jefferson's phrase, not the Constitution's) is a myth long overdue for thorough rethinking. We are deeply committed to the religion clauses of the First Amendment. They should not be understood, however, as requiring absolute separationism; such absolute separationism is theoretically inconceivable and practically contrary to the past and present interaction of church and state. It is yet another of those grand abstractions that have had such a debilitating effect upon the way society's institutions relate to one another and upon the way in which people actually order their own lives.

In brief, "no establishment of religion" should mean that no religious institution is favored by the state over other religious institutions. "Free exercise of religion" should mean that no one is forced to practice or profess any religion against his will. Where there is neither favoritism nor coercion by the state there is no violation of the separation of church and state. While the subject is more complicated than suggested here, and while the courts will no doubt take time to disentangle themselves from the confusions into which they have been led, it is to be hoped that public policy will, in general, more nearly approximate "the Kurland rule" (named after Philip Kurland of the University of Chicago), namely, that if a policy furthers a legitimate secular purpose it is a matter of legal indifference whether or not that policy employs religious institutions. Clearly, this has far-ranging implications in the areas of education, child care, and social services generally.

The danger today is not that the churches or any one church will take over the state. The much more real danger is that the state will take over the functions of the church, except for the most narrowly construed definition of religion limited to worship and religious instruction. It is not alarmist but soberly necessary to observe that the latter has been the totalitarian pattern of modern states, whether of the left or of the right. Pluralism, including religious pluralism, is one of the few strong obstacles to that pattern's success. While those who advance this pattern may often do so inadvertently, it would be naive to ignore the fact that many of them—sundry professionals, bureaucrats, politicians—have a deep vested interest in such state expansion. The interest is not only ideological, although that is no doubt the primary interest in many cases; it is also and very practically an interest in jobs and power.

From the beginning, we have emphasized the importance of mediating structures in generating and maintaining values. We have already discussed the function of the family in this connection. Within the family, and between the family and the larger society, the church is a primary agent for bearing and transmitting the operative values of our society. This is true not only in the sense that most Americans identify their most important values as being religious in character, but also in the sense that the values that inform our public discourse are inseparably related to specific religious traditions. In the absence of the church and other mediating structures that articulate these values, the result is not that the society is left without operative values; the result is that the state has an unchallenged monopoly on the generation and maintenance of values. Needless to say, we would find this a very unhappy condition indeed.

With respect to our minimalist proposition, that public policy should not undercut mediating structures, a number of implications become evident. Already mentioned are aspects of taxation and regulation, which we will treat more fully in the next section because they affect not only the church but all voluntary associations. More specific to religious institutions is the demand for "right to equal access," a notion that cannot help but undercut particularism. Here again we run into the problem of not being discriminating about discriminations or, to put it differently, of failing to distinguish between discrimination and discretion. It seems to us, for example, there is nothing wrong with an elderly Italian Roman Catholic woman wanting to live in a nursing home operated and occupied by Italian Roman Catholics. To challenge that most understandable desire seems to us, quite frankly, perverse. Yet challenged it is—indeed, it is made increasingly impossible—by depriving such a "sectarian" or "discriminatory" institution of public funds. The same obviously holds true for Methodists, atheists, Humanists, and Black Muslims. Public policy's legitimate secular purpose is to ensure that old people have proper care. It should also be public policy that such care be available as much as possible within the context that people desire for themselves and for those whom they care most about. Again, the unique proscription relevant to public policy is against racial discrimination. (To contend that, since there are few black Italian Roman Catholics or few white Black Muslims, this constitutes racial discrimination *in result* is the kind of absurd exercise in social abstraction that plagues too much policy thinking today.)

A most poignant instance of public policy's undercutting the mediating structure of religion is that of present litigation aimed at prohibiting adoption and foster-care agencies from employing a religious criterion. That is, it is proposed to outlaw agencies designed to serve Jewish, Protestant, or Catholic children, if those agencies receive public funds (which of course they do). The cruel and dehumanizing consequences of this are several. First, the parent putting a child up for adoption or surrendering a child to foster care is deprived of the most elementary say in how that child is to be reared. As mentioned in the last section, this is among the most basic of human rights and should not be denied except under the most pressing necessity, especially when one considers that the surrender of children to such agencies is not always entirely voluntary. Another consequence is that the motivation of paid and volunteer workers in such agencies is severely undercut. In many, if not most, instances that motivation is to live out and explicitly transmit religious conviction. Yet a further consequence, perhaps the most important, is that the child is deprived of religious training. This may well be construed as a denial of free exercise of religion. The state has no rightful authority to decide that this is not a serious deprivation. What is necessary to rearing the child should be left to those who bear the children and those who care for them. Except for cases of criminal neglect or other injury, the state should have no authority to intervene. Again, the legitimate secular purpose is that the children be cared for.

It might be objected that leaving such a wide range of social services to religious and other voluntary associations would mean that the many people who did not belong to such groups would go unserved. The objection is revealed as specious, however, when it is recalled that public funds would be made available to almost every conceivable kind of group so long as it were prepared to carry out the public policy purpose. Such agencies might espouse one religion, all religions, or none. Almost everyone belongs to some group that can, with public funds, facilitate public policy in the area of social services. In truth, if we are really concerned for those individuals who fall between the cracks, it is worth noting that the most anomic individuals in our society, the denizens of skid row for example, are cared for almost exclusively by voluntary associations, usually religious in character. Government bureaucracies—indeed, by definition, all bureaucracies—demonstrate little talent for helping the truly marginal who defy generalized categories. The Salvation Army needs no lessons from the state on how to be nonsectarian in its compassion for people. The raison d'être of the Salvation Army is seriously undercut, however, if its workers cannot preach to those to whom they minister.

Still on the minimalistic side of the proposition, the mediating structures paradigm opposes the growing trend toward legally enforced symbolic sterility in public space. A Christmas tree or Hanukkah lights on the town common is a good case in point. Voluntary prayer in public schools is another. "In God We Trust" inscribed on coins is another. Little things these may be, perhaps, but of myriad such little things the public ethos is formed. Reaching toward absurdity, a California court recently ruled that it was unconstitutional to have a state holiday on Good Friday. Presumably there is no objection to the previous Friday, since the secular purpose is to give another day off to state workers. But when secular purpose is combined with religious significance it is apparently beyond the pale of constitutionality.

Our proposition assumes that nobody has a right to be unaffected by the social milieu of which he or she is part. In Section II we touched on the tensions between individual and communal rights. If someone walks naked down Main Street, citizens now have the right to call in the police and have the offensive behavior stopped. Such regulations dealing with community values are of course undergoing change in many places. Change is a constant in the definition of community standards, and the authors probably tend to be more libertarian than most on the question of tolerating deviant behavior in public. The point here is that there must also be limits on the ability of individuals to call in the police to prevent behavior that is communally approved—for example, the Christmas tree on the town common. Nobody has a legal right not to encounter religious symbols in public places and thus to *impose his aversion* to such symbols on the community that cherishes them. As long as public space is open to the full range of symbols cherished in that community, there is no question of one religion being "established" over another. Public policy is presently biased toward what might be called the symbolic nakedness of the town square. Again, social abstractions have resulted in antidemocratic consequences, antidemocratic because they deny the democratically determined will of the people to celebrate themselves—their culture and their beliefs—in public, and, just as important, consequences that are antidemocratic because they give to the state a monopoly on public space and on the values to be advanced in that space.

In a public housing project in Brooklyn a deal has been struck between the leaders of a Hassidic Jewish community and of the Hispanic community to rent apartments in a way that will concentrate both communities in a more or less intact manner. The deal is probably illegal, on grounds both of racial and religious discrimination. In this particular case, it is also eminently sensible and fair, and therefore ought to be legal. No one is hurt, unless it be the "strict separationist" and "geometrical integrationist" who may be offended by the violations of their abstractions. But they are not renting apartments in public housing. We stress "in this particular case"—because public policy, especially in the area of religion and communal values, should show more respect for particular cases.

Finally, on the maximalist side of our proposition (public policy should utilize mediating structures as much as feasible) the implications spelled out throughout this essay apply also to churches. Our proposal is that the institutions of religion should be unfettered to make their maximum contribution to the public interest. In some areas of social service and education, this means these institutions should be free to continue doing what they have historically done.

Again, and in accord with our maximalist proposition, we expect increased public funding for the meeting of human needs in a wide range of policy areas; our particular contention is that mediating institutions, including religious institutions, be utilized as much as possible as the implementing agencies of policy goals. Contrary to some public policy and legal thinking today, such increased funding need not require an increase in governmental control and a consequent war on pluralism. With respect to the church and other mediating structures, the hope of the New Deal will be more nearly fulfilled when policies do not advance public compassion and responsibility at the price of conformity and repression.

V

Voluntary Association

The discussion of the church leads logically to the subject of the voluntary association. Of course the church is—in addition to whatever else it may be—a voluntary association. But the category of voluntary association includes many other structures that can play a crucial mediating role in society.

There is a history of debate over what is meant by a voluntary association. For our present purposes, a voluntary association is a body of people who have voluntarily organized themselves in pursuit of particular goals. (Following common usage, we exclude business corporations and other primarily economic associations.) Important to the present discussion is the subject of volunteer service. Many voluntary associations have both paid and volunteer staffing. For our purposes, the crucial point is the free association of people for some collective purpose, the fact that they may pay some individuals for doing work to this end not being decisive.

At least since de Tocqueville the importance of voluntary associations in American democracy has been widely recognized. Voluntarism has flourished in America more than in any other Western society and it is reasonable to believe this may have something to do with American political institutions. Associations create statutes, elect officers, debate, vote courses of action, and otherwise serve as schools for democracy. However trivial, wrongheaded, or bizarre we may think the purpose of some associations to be, they nonetheless perform this vital function.

Apart from this political role, voluntary associations are enormously important for what they have actually done. Before the advent of the modern welfare state, almost everything in the realm of social services was under the aegis of voluntary associations, usually religious in character. Still today there are about 1,900 private colleges and universities, 4,600 private secondary schools, 3,600 voluntary hospitals, 6,000 museums, 1,100 orchestras, 5,500 libraries, and no less than 29,000 nongovernmental welfare agencies. Of course not all of these are equally important as mediating structures. Orchestras and groups promoting stamp-collecting or the preservation of antique automobiles are, however important in other connections, outside our focus here. We are interested in one type within the vast array of voluntary associations—namely, associations that render social services relevant to recognized public responsibilities.

Assaults on voluntary associations come from several directions, from both the right and left of the political spectrum. Some condemn them as inefficient, corrupt, divisive, and even subversive. Many subscribe to the axiom that public services should not be under private control. From the far left comes the challenge that such associations supply mere palliatives, perpetuate the notion of charity, and otherwise manipulate people into acceptance of the status quo.

Such assaults are not merely verbal. They reflect a trend to establish a state monopoly over all organized activities that have to do with more than strictly private purposes. This trend has borne fruit in outright prohibition, in repressive taxation, and in the imposition of licensing and operating standards that have a punitive effect on nongovernmental agencies.

Of course there are instances of corruption and inefficiency in voluntary agencies. A comparison of governmental and nongovernmental social services on these scores, however, hardly supports the case for governmental monopoly. It should be obvious that government bureaucrats have a vested interest in maintaining and expanding government monopolies. Similarly, politicians have an interest in setting up services for which they can claim credit and over which they can exercise a degree of power. In short, social services in the modern welfare state are inescapably part of the political pork barrel.

Pork barrels may be necessary to political democracy. The problem confronting us arises when the vested interests in question use coercive state power to repress individual freedom, initiative, and social diversity. We are not impressed by the argument that this is necessary because voluntary associations often overlap with the functions of government agencies. Overlap may in fact provide creative competition, incentives for performance, and increased choice. But our more basic contention is against the notion that anything public must *ipso facto* be governmental. That notion is profoundly contrary to the American political tradition and is, in its consequences, antidemocratic. It creates clients of the state instead of free citizens. It stifles the initiative and responsibility essential to the life of the polity.

Our present problem is also closely linked with the trend toward professionalization. Whether in government or nongovernment agencies, professionals attack allegedly substandard services, and substandard generally means nonprofessional. Through organizations and lobbies, professionals increasingly persuade the state to legislate standards and certifications that hit voluntary associations hard, especially those given to employing volunteers. The end result is that the trend toward government monopoly operates in tandem with the trend toward professional monopoly over social services. The connection between such monopoly control and the actual quality of services delivered is doubtful indeed.

Professional standards are of course important in some areas. But they must be viewed with robust skepticism when expertise claims jurisdiction, as it were, over the way people run their own lives. Again, ordinary people are the best experts on themselves. Tutelage by certified experts is bad enough when exercised by persuasion—as, for example, when parents are so demoralized that they feel themselves incapable of raising their children without ongoing reference to child-raising experts. It is much worse, however, when such tutelage is imposed coercively. And, of course, lower-income people are most effectively disfranchised by the successful establishment of expert monopolies.

Professionalization is now being exacerbated by unionization of professionals. In principle, employees of nongovernment agencies can be unionized as readily as government employees. In practice, large unions prefer to deal with the large and unified management that government offers. Standards and certification become items of negotiation between union and management, thus reinforcing the drive toward professional monopolies. In addition, unions would seem to have an intrinsic antagonism toward volunteer work. It is alleged that the volunteer is an unpaid laborer and is therefore exploited. This argument has been recently advanced also by some feminists, since many volunteers are women.

In protesting the use of labor and feminist rhetoric to camouflage the establishment of coercive monopolies and the disfranchisement of people in the running of their own lives, our position is neither anti-union nor anti-feminist. Who defines exploitation? We trust people to know when they are being exploited, without the benefit of instruction by professionals, labor organizers, or feminist authors. So long as voluntary work is genuinely voluntary—is undertaken by free choice—it should be cherished and not maligned. It is of enormous value in terms of both the useful activity offered to volunteers and the actual services rendered. In addition, because of their relative freedom from bureaucratic controls, voluntary associations are important laboratories of innovation in social services; and, of course, they sustain the expression of the rich pluralism of American life.

Attacks on the volunteer principle also aid the expansion of the kind of capitalist mentality that would put a dollar sign on everything on the grounds that only that which has a price tag has worth. We believe it proper and humane (as well as "human") that there be areas of life, including public life, in which there is not a dollar sign on everything. It is debilitating to our sense of the polity to assume that only private life is to be governed by humane, nonpecuniary motives, while the rest of life is a matter of dog-eat-dog.

An additional word should be said about the development of paraprofessional fields. To be sure, people who make their living in any socially useful occupation should be given respectful recognition and should be paid a decent wage. However, much of the paraprofessional development is in fact empire-building by professional and union monopolists who would incorporate lower-status occupations into their hierarchy. At least in some instances, the word that best describes this development is exploitation. This is the case, for example, when parents and other lay people can no longer hold professionals to account because they have themselves been co-opted into the vested interests of the professionals.

With the immense growth of knowledge and skills in modern society, professions are necessary and it is inevitable that there be organizations and unions to defend their interests. This development cannot be, and should not be, reversed. It can, however, be redirected. The purpose of the professions is to serve society—not the other way around. Too often professionals regard those they serve as clients in the rather unfortunate sense the Latin word originally implied. The clients of a Roman patrician were one step above his slaves in the social hierarchy, not entirely unlike some of today's servile dependents upon professionals. Such a notion has no place in democratic society.

Professionals should be ancillary to the people they serve. Upper-income people refer to "our" doctor or "my" doctor, and whatever patterns of dependency they develop are largely of their own choosing. It should be possible for lower-income people to use the possessive pronoun in referring to professionals.

The policy implications of our approach touch also on the role of nonprofit foundations in our society. Technically, there are different kinds of foundations—strictly private, publicly supported, operating, and so on—but the current assault applies to all of them. The argument is summed up in the words of the late Wright Patman whose crusade against foundations led to Title I of the Tax Reform Act of 1969:

> Today I shall introduce a bill to end a gross inequity which this country and its citizens can no longer afford: the tax-exempt status of the so-called privately controlled charitable foundations, and their propensity for domination of business and accumulation of wealth. . . . Put most bluntly, philanthropy—one of mankind's more noble instincts—has been perverted into a vehicle for institutionalized deliberate evasion of fiscal and moral responsibility to the nation. *(Congressional Record,* August 6, 1969)

Of course, foundations have engaged in abuses that need to be curbed, but the resentment and hostility manifested by the curbers also needs to be curbed if we are not to harm the society very severely. The curbers of foundations make up an odd coalition. Right-wing forces are hostile to foundations because of their social experimentation (such as the Ford Foundation's programs among inner-city blacks), while others are hostile because of the role of big business ("the establishment") in funding foundations. The most dangerous part of the 1969 legislation is the new power given to the

Internal Revenue Service to police foundation activities. The power to revoke or threaten to revoke tax exemption is a most effective instrument of control. (In recent years such threats have been made against religious organizations that opposed the Vietnam War and advocated sundry unpopular causes.) More ominous than the prospect that a few millionaires will get away with paying less taxes is the prospect of government control over officially disapproved advocacy or programs.

Directly related to this concern is the relatively new concept of tax expenditure that has been infiltrated into public policy. It is calculated, for example, that a certain amount of revenue is lost to the government because a private college is tax exempt. The revenue lost is called a tax expenditure. This may seem like an innocuous bit of bookkeeping, but the term expenditure implies that the college is in fact government-subsidized (a tax expenditure is a kind of government expenditure) and therefore ought to be governmentally controlled. This implication, which is made quite explicit by some bureaucrats, is incipiently totalitarian. The logic is that all of society's wealth *really* belongs to the government and that the government should therefore be able to determine how all wealth— including the wealth exempted from taxation—should be used. The concept of tax expenditure should be used, if at all, as a simple accounting device having no normative implications.

While large foundations would seem to be remote from the mediating structures under discussion, in fact they are often important to such structures at the most local level, especially in the areas of education and health. Were all these institutions taken over by the government, there might be a more uniform imposition of standards and greater financial accountability than now exists (although the monumental corruption in various government social services does not make one sanguine about the latter), but the price would be high. Massive bureaucratization, the proliferation of legal procedures that generate both public resentment and business for lawyers, the atrophying of the humane impulse, the increase of alienation—these would be some of the costs. Minimally, it should be public policy to encourage the voluntarism that, in our society, has at least slowed down these costs of modernity.

As always, the maximalist side of our approach—that is, using voluntary associations as agents of public policies—is more problematic than the minimalist. One thinks, for example, of the use of foster homes and half-way houses in the treatment and prevention of drug addiction, juvenile delinquency, and mental illness. There is reason to believe such approaches are both less costly and more effective than using bureaucratized megastructures (and their local outlets). Or one thinks of the successful resettlement of more than 100,000 Vietnam refugees in 1975, accomplished not by setting up a government agency but by working through voluntary agencies (mainly religious). This instance of using voluntary associations for public policy purposes deserves careful study. Yet another instance is the growth of the women's health movement, which in some areas is effectively challenging the monopolistic practices of the medical establishment. The ideas of people such as Ivan Illich and Victor Fuchs should be examined for their potential to empower people to reassume responsibility for their own health care. Existing experiments in decentralizing medical delivery systems should also be encouraged, with a view toward moving from decentralization to genuine empowerment.

We well know that proposals for community participation are not new. The most obvious example is the Community Action Program (CAP), a part of the War Against Poverty of the 1960s. CAP led to much disillusionment. Some condemned it as a mask for co-opting those who did, or might, threaten local power elites. Thus, community organizations were deprived of real potency and turned into government dependents. From the other side of the political spectrum, CAP was condemned for funding agitators and subversives. Yet others charged that CAP pitted community organizations against the institutions of representative government. To some extent these criticisms are mutually exclusive—they cannot all be true simultaneously. Yet no doubt all these things happened in various places in the 1960s.

That experience in no way invalidates the idea of community participation. First, the peculiar developments of the 1960s made that decade the worst possible time to try out the idea (and the same might be said about experiments in the community control of schools during the same period). Second, and much more important, the institutions used to facilitate community participation were not the actual institutions of the community but were created by those in charge of the program. This was especially true in inner-city black areas—the chief focus of the program—where religious institutions were, for the most part, neglected or even deliberately undercut. So, to some extent, were the family structures of the black community. In short, the program's failures resulted precisely from its failure to utilize existing mediating structures.

This said, it remains true that mediating structures can be co-opted by government, that they can become instruments of those interested in destroying rather than reforming American society, and that they can undermine the institutions of the formal polity. These are real risks. On the other side are the benefits described earlier. Together they constitute a major challenge to the political imagination.

VI

Empowerment through Pluralism

T he theme of pluralism has recurred many times in this essay. This final section aims simply to tie up a few loose ends, to anticipate some objections to a public policy designed to sustain pluralism through mediating structures, and to underscore some facts of *American* society that suggest both the potentials and limitations of the approach advanced here.

It should be obvious that by pluralism we mean much more than regional accents, St. Patrick's Day, and Black Pride Days, as important as all these are. Beyond providing the variety of color, costume, and custom, pluralism makes possible a tension within worlds and between worlds of meaning. Worlds of meaning put reality together in a distinctive way. Whether the participants in these worlds see themselves as mainline or subcultural, as establishment or revolutionary, they are each but part of the cultural whole. Yet the paradox is that wholeness is experienced through affirmation of the part in which one participates. This relates to the aforementioned insight of Burke regarding "the little platoon." In more contemporary psychological jargon it relates to the "identity crisis" which results from an "identity diffusion" in mass society. Within one's group—whether it be racial, national, political, religious, or all of these—one discovers an answer to the elementary question, "Who am I?" and is supported in living out that answer. Psychologically and sociologically, we would propose the axiom that any identity is better than none. Politically, we would argue that it is not the business of public policy to make value judgments regarding the merits or demerits of various identity solutions, so long as all groups abide by the minimal rules that make a pluralistic society possible. It is the business of public policy not to undercut, and indeed to enhance, the identity choices available to theAmerican people (our minimalist and maximalist propositions throughout).

This approach assumes that the process symbolized by "E Pluribus Unum" is not a zero-sum game. That is, the *unum is* not to be achieved at the expense of the *plures.* To put it positively, the national purpose indicated by the *unum is* precisely to sustain the *plures.* Of course there are tensions, and accommodations are necessary if the structures necessary to national existence are to be maintained. But in the art of pluralistic politics, such tensions are not to be eliminated but are to be welcomed as the catalysts of more imaginative accommodations. Public policy in the areas discussed in this essay has in recent decades, we believe, been too negative in its approach to the tensions of diversity and therefore too ready to impose uniform solutions on what are perceived as national social problems. In this approach, pluralism is viewed as an enemy of social policy planning rather than as a source of more diversified solutions to problems that are, after all, diversely caused and diversely defined.

Throughout this essay, we have emphasized that our proposal contains no animus toward those charged with designing and implementing social policy nor any indictment of their good intentions. The reasons for present pluralism-eroding policies are to be discovered in part in the very processes implicit in the metaphors of modernization, rationalization, and bureaucratization. The management mindset of the megastructure—whether of HEW, Sears Roebuck, or the AFL-CIO—is biased toward the unitary solution. The neat and comprehensive answer is impatient of "irrational" particularities and can only be forced to yield to greater nuance when it encounters resistance, whether from the economic market of consumer wants or from the political market of organized special interest groups. The challenge of public policy is to anticipate such resistance and, beyond that, to cast aside its adversary posture toward particularism and embrace as its goal the advancement of the multitude of particular interests that in fact constitute the common weal. Thus, far from denigrating social planning, our proposal challenges the policy maker with a much more complicated and exciting task than today's approach. Similarly, the self-esteem of the professional in all areas of social service is elevated when he or she defines the professional task in terms of being helpful and ancillary to people rather than in terms of creating a power monopoly whereby people become dependent clients.

Of course, some critics will decry our proposal as "balkanization," "retribalization," "parochialization," and such. The relevance of the Balkan areas aside, we want frankly to assert that tribe and parochial are not terms of derision. That they are commonly used in a derisive manner is the result of a world view emerging from the late eighteenth century. That world view held, in brief, that the laws of Nature are reflected in a political will of the people that can be determined and implemented by rational persons. Those naive notions of Nature, Will, and Reason have in the last hundred years been thoroughly discredited in almost every discipline, from psychology to sociology to physics. Yet the irony is that, although few people still believe in these myths, most social thought and planning continues to act as though they were true. The result is that the enemies of particularism ("tribalism") have become an elite tribe attempting to impose order on the seeming irrationalities of the real world and operating on premises that most Americans find both implausible and hostile to their values. Social thought has been crippled and policies have miscarried because we have not developed a paradigm of pluralism to replace the discredited assumptions of the eighteenth century. We hope this proposal is one step toward developing such a paradigm.

Throughout this essay we have frequently referred to democratic values and warned against their authoritarian and totalitarian alternatives. We are keenly aware of the limitations in any notion of "the people" actually exercising the *kratein,* the effective authority, in public policy. And we are keenly aware of how far the American polity is from demonstrating what is possible in the democratic idea. The result of political manipulation, media distortion, and the sheer weight of indifference is that the great majority of Americans have little or no political will, in the sense that term is used in democratic theory, on the great questions of domestic and international policy. Within the formal framework of democratic polity, these questions will perforce be answered by a more politicized elite. But it is precisely with respect to mediating structures that most people do have, in the most exact sense, a political will. On matters of family, church, neighborhood, hobbies, working place, and recreation, most people have a very clear idea of what is in their interest. If we are truly committed to the democratic process, it is *their* political will that public policy should be designed to empower. It may be lamentable that most Americans have no political will with respect to U.S. relations with Brazil, but that is hardly reason to undercut their very clear political will about how their children should be educated. Indeed policies that disable political will where it does exist preclude the development of political will where it does not now exist, thus further enfeebling the democratic process and opening the door to its alternatives.

As difficult as it may be for some to accept, all rational interests do not converge—or at least there is no universal agreement on what interests are rational. This means that public policy must come to terms with perduring contradictions. We need not resign ourselves to the often cynically invoked axiom that "politics is the art of the possible." In fact politics is the art of discovering *what* is possible. The possibility to be explored is not how far unitary policies can be extended before encountering the backlash of particularity. Rather, the possibility to be explored is how a common purpose can be achieved through the enhancement of myriad particular interests. This requires a new degree of modesty among those who think about social policy—not modesty in the sense of lowering our ideals in the search for meeting human needs and creating a more just society, but modesty about *our* definitions of need and justice. Every world within this society, whether it calls itself a subculture or a supraculture or simply the American culture, is in fact a subculture, is but a part of the whole. This fact needs to be systematically remembered among those who occupy the world of public policy planning and implementation.

The subculture that envisages its values as universal and its style as cosmopolitan is no less a subculture for all that. The tribal patterns evident at an Upper West Side cocktail party are no less tribal than those evident at a Polish dance in Greenpoint, Brooklyn. That the former is produced by the interaction of people trying to transcend many particularisms simply results in a new, and not necessarily more interesting, particularism. People at the cocktail party may think of themselves as liberated, and indeed they may have elected to leave behind certain particularisms into which they were born. They have, in effect, elected a new particularism. *Lib-*

eration is not escape from particularity but discovery of the particularity that fits. Elected particularities may include life style, ideology, friendships, place of residence, and so forth. Inherited particularities may include race, economic circumstance, region, religion, and, in most cases, politics. Pluralism means the lively interaction among inherited particularities and, through election, the evolution of new particularities. The goal of public policy in a pluralistic society is to sustain as many particularities as possible, in the hope that most people will accept, discover, or devise one that fits.

It might be argued that the redirection of public policy proposed here is in fact naive and quixotic. A strong argument can be made that the dynamics of modernity, operating through the megastructures and especially through the modern state, are like a great leviathan or steamroller, inexorably destroying every obstacle that gets in the way of creating mass society. There is much and ominous evidence in support of that argument. While we cannot predict the outcome of this process, we must not buckle under to alleged inevitabilities. On the more hopeful side are indications that the political will of the American people is beginning to assert itself more strongly in resistance to "massification." In contradiction of social analysts who describe the irresistible and homogenizing force of the communications media, for example, there is strong evidence that the media message is not received uncritically but is refracted through myriad world views that confound the intentions of would-be manipulators of the masses. (Happily, there are also many often-contradictory media messages.) New "Edsels" still get rejected (though the Edsel itself is a collector's item). The antiwar bias of much news about the Vietnam War (a bias we shared) was, studies suggest, often refracted in a way that reinforced support of official policy. Promotion of diverse sexual and life-style liberations seems to be doing little empirically verifiable damage to devotion to the family ideal. Thirty years of network TV English (not to mention thirty years of radio before that) has hardly wiped out regional dialect. In short, and to the consternation of political, cultural, and commercial purveyors of new soaps, the American people demonstrate a robust skepticism toward the modern peddlers of new worlds and a remarkable inclination to trust their own judgments. We do not wish to exaggerate these signs of hope. Counter-indicators can be listed in abundance. We do suggest there is no reason to resign ourselves to the "massification" that is so often described as America today.

America today—those words are very important to our argument. While our proposal is, we hope, relevant to modern industrialized society in general, whether socialist or capitalist, its possibilities are peculiarly attuned to the United States. (We might say, to North America, including Canada, but some aspects of particularism in Canada—for example, binationalism between French- and English-speaking Canadians—are beyond the scope of this essay.) There are at least five characteristics of American society that make it the most likely laboratory for public policy designed to enhance mediating structures and the pluralism that mediating structures make possible. First is the immigrant nature of American society. The implications of that fact for pluralism need no elaboration. Second, ours is a relatively affluent society. We have the resources to experiment toward a more humane order—for example, to place a floor of economic decency under every American. Third, this is a relatively stable society. Confronted by the prospects of neither revolution nor certain and rapid decline, we do not face the crises that call for total or definitive answers to social problems. Fourth, American society is effectively pervaded by the democratic idea and by the sense of tolerance and fair play that make the democratic process possible. This makes our society ideologically hospitable to pluralism. And fifth, however weakened they may be, we still have relatively strong institutions—political, economic, religious, and cultural—that supply countervailing forces in the shaping of social policy. Aspirations toward monopoly can, at least in theory, be challenged. And our history demonstrates that the theory has, more often than not, been acted out in practice.

Finally, we know there are those who contend that, no matter how promising all this may be for America, America is very bad for the rest of the world. It is argued that the success of America's experiment in democratic pluralism is at the expense of others, especially at the expense of the poorer nations. It is a complicated argument to which justice cannot be done here. But it might be asked, in turn, whether America would in some sense be better for the world were we to eliminate any of the five characteristics mentioned above. Were the American people more homogeneous, were they as poor as the peasants of Guatemala, were their institutions less stable and their democratic impulses less ingrained—would any of these conditions contribute concretely to a more just global order? We think not.

Neither, on the other hand, are we as convinced as some others seem to be that America is the "advance society" of human history, or at least of the modern industrialized world. Perhaps it is—perhaps not. But of *this* we are convinced: America has a singular opportunity to contest the predictions of the inevitability of mass society with its anomic individuals, alienated and impotent, excluded from the ordering of a polity that is no longer theirs. And we are convinced that mediating structures might be the agencies for a new empowerment of people in America's renewed experiment in democratic pluralism.

Notes

CHAPTER 1: INTRODUCTION, *Michael Novak*

1. The other four volumes in the series, whose completion Woodson also helped supervise, were *The Hidden Health Care System: Mediating Structures and Medicine,* edited by Lowell S. Levin and Ellen L. Idler; *Housing and Public Policy: A Role for Mediating Structures*, edited by John Eagan, John Carr, Andrew Mott, and John Roos; *Mediating Structures and Welfare*, edited by Nathan Glazer; and *Mediating Structures and Education*, edited by David Seeley.

CHAPTER 2: A NEW CIVIC LIFE,
Michael S. Joyce and William A. Schambra

1. Robert Wiebe, *The Search for Order, 1877 to 1920* (New York: Hill and Wang, 1967).

2. Robert A. Nisbet, *The Quest for Community* (Oxford: Oxford University Press, 1971), p. 54.

3. Alexis de Tocqueville, *Democracy in America* (Garden City, N.Y.: Doubleday, 1969), p. 513.

4. Walter Lippman, *Drift and Mastery* (Englewood Cliffs, N.J.: Prentice Hall, Inc., 1961), p. 81.

5. John Dewey, *The Public and Its Problems: An Essay in Political Inquiry* (Chicago: Gateway Books, 1946), p. 98.

6. Charles Horton Cooley, *Social Process* (New York: Charles Scribner's Sons, 1918), p. 347.

7. Frederick C. Howe, *Wisconsin: An Experiment in Democracy* (New York: Charles Scribner's Sons, 1912), p. 38.

8. Timothy Kaufman-Osborn, "John Dewey and the Liberal Science

of Community," *Journal of Politics,* vol. 46 (November 1984), p. 1157.

9. Samuel Hayes, "The Politics of Reform in Municipal Government in the Progressive Era," *Pacific Northwest Quarterly,* October 1964.

10. Sol Cohen, quoted in Joel H. Spring, *Education and the Rise of the Corporate State* (Boston: Beacon Press, 1972), p. 87.

11. Ibid.

12. John Bascom, quoted in J. D. Hoeveler, "The University and the Social Gospel: The Intellectual Origins of the 'Wisconsin Idea,'" *Wisconsin Magazine of History,* vol. 59 (Summer 1976), p. 288.

13. Ibid., p. 292.

14. Robert Park, *The City* (Chicago: University of Chicago Press, 1967), p. 107.

15. Samuel Beer, "In Search of New Public Philosophy," in *The New American Political System*, ed. Anthony King (Washington, D.C.: American Enterprise Institute, 1978), p. 8 (footnote).

16. Stokely Carmichael and Charles V. Hamilton, *Black Power: The Politics of Liberation in America* (New York: Random House, 1967).

17. Robert F. Kennedy, *To Seek a Newer World* (Garden City, N.Y.: Doubleday, 1967).

18. Novak, ibid., p. 273.

19. George Wallace, quoted in Michael Novak, *The Rise of the Unmeltable Ethnics: Politics and Culture in the Seventies* (New York: Macmillan, 1972), pp. 135–66.

20. Michael Sandel, "This Election Was Haunted by the Fear That We Are Losing Control," *New York Times,* November 10, 1994.

CHAPTER 4: MEDIATING STRUCTURES, 1977–1995, *James P. Pinkerton*

1. Peggy Noonan, Interview, April 10, 1995.

2. William J. Bennett, *Index of Leading Cultural Indicators* (New York: Touchstone, 1994), p. 8.

CHAPTER 7: PHILANTHROPY AND THE WELFARE STATE, *Leslie Lenkowsky*

1. "Republicans' Welfare Reform Could Be Charities' Burden," *The Chronicle of Philanthropy*, November 29, 1994, pp. 6–7; Henry Goldstein, "Voters' Mandate to Punish Society's Victims," ibid., pp. 39–40.

2. As Waldemar A. Nielsen has pointed out, even in the nineteenth century, government provided financial support to charities. Such grants were generally to assist the initiatives (and priorities) of the charities, however, not for the purpose of implementing a government program. Compare Waldemar A. Nielsen, *The Endangered Sector* (New York: Columbia University Press), 1979, pp. 25–48.

3. Dwight F. Burlingame, ed., *The Responsibilities of Wealth* (Indianapolis: Indiana University Press, 1992), pp. 15–26.

4. The Commission on Foundations and Private Philanthropy, *Foundations, Private Giving, and Public Policy* (Chicago: University of Chicago Press), 1970, p. 20.

5. Lester M. Salamon, "Rethinking Public Management: Third-Party Government and the Changing Forms of Government Action," *Public Policy*, vol. 29 (1981), pp. 255–75.

6. This was an outgrowth of the growing professionalization of philanthropy, which had seen both charities and grant-making foundations replace the generalists and volunteers who had run them in the past with specialists and paid staff, usually drawn from the universities. The 1969 tax act, as well as the expansion of government support for nonprofits, gave further impetus to this trend.

7. Commission on Private Philanthropy and Public Needs, *Giving in America: Toward a Stronger Voluntary Sector,* 1975, p. 89.

8. "Non-Profit Executives Get 6.4% Increase in Pay," *Chronicle of Philanthropy,* October 4, 1994, p. 45. Only the chief executive officer, deputy executive officer, and top legal position received a larger average salary.

9. Conversely, those nonprofits that are least likely to be involved in the "partnership," such as religious schools, seem to have had better results in developing programs that, for example, work with children from disadvantaged backgrounds.

10. Among the more notable results of such efforts are public television, the War on Poverty's Community Action Program, federal funding for the arts, President Carter's energy program, and a variety of attempts to encourage the spread of health maintenance organizations and other forms of managed care.

11. For want of a better word, these ideas could be called "liberal" inasmuch as they generally correspond to what are usually seen as liberal ideas about public policy. Their roots, however, lie less in common political convictions than in common training, particularly in universities and professional schools, and career paths, including more than a little movement between government and nonprofit jobs.

12. Lester M. Salamon with Alan J. Abramson, *The Federal Government and the Nonprofit Secotr: Implications of the Reagan Budget Proposals* (Washington, D.C.: Urban Institute, 1981); Lester M. Salamon and Alan J. Abramson, *The Federal Budget and the Nonprofit Sector* (Washington, D.C.: Urban Institute, 1982); Alan J. Abramson and Lester M. Salamon, *The Nonprofit Sector and the New Federal Budget* (Washington, D.C.: Urban Institute, 1986).

13. Alan J. Abramson, Lester M. Salamon, and C. Eugene Steuerle, *The Nonprofit Sector and the Federal Budget in the 1990s* (Washington, D.C.: Urban Institute), February 1994, unpublished.

14. This would include federal support for income assistance, for example, which is paid directly to the recipient. It is not obvious that

nonprofits should be expected to replace any shortfall in these programs with private revenues.

15. Or writers about it. Compare "The Myths of Charity," *U.S. News and World Report,* January 16, 1995, pp. 39–40.

CHAPTER 8: RELIGIOUS CHARITIES,   *Marvin Olasky*

1. See Marvin Olasky, *The Tragedy of American Compassion* (Washington, D.C.: Regnery, 1992).

2. Lynn Buzzard and Susan Edwards, *Risky Business* (Ann Arbor, Mich.: J.W. Edwards, 1994), sect. A–2, p. 26.

3. Some 57 percent of the organization's income for 1993 came directly from government agencies, and 17 percent indirectly (through management for transitional housing, with fees paid by other nonprofits from government funds). Only 26 percent came from private or church contributions.

4. Maria Velez, interview with the author, 1993.

5. Bob Schwab, interview with the author, 1992 and 1993.

6. Alton Dyer, interview with the author, 1992.

7. Ibid.

8. Schwab interview.

9. Gary Thornton, interview with the author, 1992. Documents filed with the Texas secretary of state show HOBO's change in orientation. On September 11, 1987, HOBO received a certificate of incorporation noting that "the property, assets, profits and net income of this corporation are irrevocably dedicated to religious purposes." The papers also note that if HOBO folded, its assets were to be distributed to an organization operated "exclusively for religious purposes." Two years later, the board of directors amended HOBO's articles of incorporation to revoke the irrevocable dedication; the board deleted "religious purposes" and replaced those words with "charitable purposes."

10. John Porterfield, interview with the author, 1992.

11. Marion Coleman, interview with the author, 1992.

12. Marion Morris, interview with the author, 1992.

13. Ibid.

14. Barney O'Connor, interview with the author, 1992.

15. Press release supplied by HOBO.

CHAPTER 11: BOTTOM-UP FUNDING,   *Douglas J. Besharov*

1. Allan Meltzer, "Why Governments Make Bad Venture Capitalists," *Wall Street Journal,* May 5, 1993.

2. I return to this important point in the conclusion.

3. This issue is widely discussed in the academic literature concerning the "implementation" of social programs. See, for example, Paul

Sabatier, "Top-down and Bottom-up Approach to Implementation Research: A Critical Analysis and Suggested Synthesis," *Journal of Public Policy*, vol. 6, no. 1 (1986), pp. 21–48; Dennis Palumbo, "Symposium: Implementation, What We Have Learned and Still Need to Know," *Policy Studies Review Annual*, vol. 7, no. 1 (1987), pp. 91–102.

4. Usually the money moves from the federal government to a state government and then to service providers, but this chapter's argument is independent of issues of federalism. The same three axioms apply to state- and locally funded programs.

5. For brevity of presentation, I have treated a tax cut as cash assistance, even though it is the taxpayer's own money that is involved.

6. Eugene Steuerle, "The Tax Treatment of Households of Different Size," in *Taxing the Family*, Rudolph Penner, ed. (Washington, D.C.: AEI Press, 1983), pp. 73–97; Eugene Steuerle and Jason Juffras, "A $1,000 Tax Credit for Every Child: A Base of Reform for the Nation's Tax, Welfare, and Health Systems," Urban Institute Policy Paper (Washington, D.C., April 1991).

7. Douglas J. Besharov and John C. Weicher, "Return the Family to 1954," *Wall Street Journal*, July 8, 1985.

8. See, for instance, Eugene Steuerle, "Is There a Filing Season Foulup? What's Not Being Said," *Tax Notes*, March 13, 1995, pp. 1709–10; Eugene Steuerle, "The IRS Cannot Control the New Superterranean Economy," *Tax Notes*, June 29, 1993, pp. 1839–40.

9. Hence, deciding to use a voucher scheme requires a prediction of the degree to which they can be sold or traded and then deciding if the predicted level of abuse is acceptable.

10. Christopher Jencks, *The Homeless* (Cambridge: Harvard University Press, 1994), pp. 107–22.

11. This chapter does not endorse total reimbursement schemes, such as Medicaid and Medicare; although they maximize client choice, they do not provide sufficient incentives for recipients to constrain costs.

12. Because each approach relies on individual decision making, they all would probably survive the challenge that they provide an aid to religion.

Index

Abortion services, 131
Abramson, Alan J., 92
Acton (lord), 35, 139
Adoption policies, 190
Aid to Families with Dependent
  Children (AFDC), 127, 129
Akers, John, 57
Alcohol addiction, 110–12, 114
Alcoholics Anonymous, 120
Alienation, 159, 162, 167
Alinsky, Saul, 55
Alum Rock, California, 182
American Civil Liberties Union, 74
American Federation of Teachers,
  73, 183
AmeriCorps, 56
Anarcho-syndicalism, 160, 162
Ancient Order of Foresters, 38
Anderson, Martin, 54
Aristotle, 34, 35, 62, 153
Association principle, 8, 140
Associations, 159
  British experience, 4, 30, 37–43
  institutional roles, 30–33, 47–48,
    87, 117, 138, 194–201
  professionalization, 196–98

tax-exempt status controversy,
  198–99
volunteer principle attacked, 197
See also specific associations
Authoritarianism, 35, 178

Ballots, 16
Bandow, Douglas, 54
Baroni, Gino, 53
Bascom, John, 17, 18
Beer, Samuel, 19
Bennett, William, 55
Berger, Brigitta, 107
Berger, Peter L., 1, 2, 8, 29, 52–53,
  55, 57, 107, 145–54
Besharov, Douglas, 7, 124–31, 151
Black Power (Carmichael and Ham-
  ilton), 21
Black Power movement, 21
Block grants, 23, 24, 117
Boot camps, 107
Boy Scouts, 138
Brennan, William, 71, 80
Britain, 140, 180
  private welfare experience, 4, 37–
    43

A NOTE ON THE BOOK

This book was edited by Dana Lane
of the publications staff
of the American Enterprise Institute.
The index was prepared by Patricia Ruggiero.
The text was set in New Century Schoolbook.
Lisa Roman of the AEI Press set the type,
and Data Reproductions Corporation,
of Rochester Hills, Michigan,
printed and bound the book,
using permanent acid-free paper.

The AEI Press is the publisher for the American Enterprise Institute for Public Policy Research, 1150 Seventeenth Street, N.W., Washington, D.C. 20036; *Christopher C. DeMuth,* publisher; *Dana Lane,* director; *Ann Petty,* editor; *Leigh Tripoli,* editor; *Cheryl Weissman,* editor; *Lisa Roman,* editorial assistant (rights and permissions).